Praise for *Well, Girl*

"It's like Jami (without an 'e') stepped into my ginormous size 11 Birkenstock sandals and wrote this book just for me. Like most women, I've struggled with self-confidence most of my life. I'm too loud, too tall, † ̣de, my hair is too frizzy in humidity, just 'too'— but she has written a h   ̣redibly insightful, and wisdom-laden book to remind us all tha†   much for our Savior. Our self-worth lies in Him alone. Thi̕   ̣y woman."

–Susannah B. Lewis, Whoa Sus̕   ̣his Stuff Up

"Are you weighed down by an   ̣. Has a fixation on your appearance turned ug   ̣oid exercise? What if I told you, you can be done w̕   ̣om the inside out? Find lighthearted freedom from the sc̕   ̣ame as you step into all God has for you, without counting calor̕   ̣g carbs. It's time to be well, girl. You'll never be the same!"

–Katie M. Reid, pear-shaped body, liberated heart, and author of *Made Like Martha*

"My own struggle with body image has been real, but Jami Amerine's trademark mix of humorous personal stories and grace-based advice has helped me make peace with my pounds. Thanks to Jami, I've switched my focus from what mirrors reveal about me to how my Maker rejoices in me. She's helped me see that true wellness can never be found in trendy dietary fads but only in the opinions of our timeless, devoted Father. It's time to step off the scale and dine on the scriptures within this book. For if our diet is full of their truth, then we will be well, girls, and able to feast on both carrots AND Cheetos with confidence and joy."

–Tracy Steel, speaker and author of *A Redesigned Life: Uncovering God's Purpose When Life Doesn't Go as Planned*

"*Well, Girl* is not like any other wellness book. You know, the ones with the typical (and exhausting) advice of 'exercise and food measuring' routines. Instead, *Well, Girl* is an encounter with who we are and how much we are loved—a completely different way to look at health. Even more, it's an invitation to unravel the lies that have kept us tangled in bad choices. It's an invitation to change from the inside out, and finally be completely free. Amerine is a brilliant author who walks out her messages. She is funny, honest, and a lover of Jesus. Let her words soak into your weary soul."

–Carey Scott, author of *Uncommon* and *Unafraid*

"*Well, Girl* is a feast of freedom and grace with heaping side orders of joy and laughter. If you have a love-hate relationship with food and your body, or if you have secretly pictured God as the Great Food Judge in the Sky, constantly changing his approval of you based on how you eat and what you weigh, get ready to be set free. Jami doesn't tell you what to do; she reminds you who you are—and who God is. *Well, Girl* isn't just a book on wellness; it's a banquet for the soul."

–Elizabeth Laing Thompson, author of *When God Says, "Wait," When God Says, "Go,"* and *All the Feels*

"Jami brings humor, transparency, and heart to this beautiful book. She bravely shares personal disappointments and insightful revelations on the journey to inner wellness. She challenges you to examine your beliefs and align them with the grace that is offered through Jesus Christ. She is clear about being on the journey with you and offers her experience and encouragement that will lift you up and give you confidence. Jami's words release you from the shame of self-sabotage and empower you to embrace who God made you to be. Grab your tissues as you sit down with a friend who will inspire you to know God in deeper ways."

–Jill Monaco, Founder and President of Jill Monaco Ministries

"*Well, Girl* is a sacred journey of freedom for all women who have struggled with their bodies, food, striving to be better, and accepting themselves as is. As a counselor and overcomer of disordered eating myself, I love the perspective of being a whole woman Jami provides!"

–Brenda L. Yoder, counselor, speaker, and author
of *Fledge: Launching Your Kids Without Losing Your Mind*

"With grace, truth, and a lot of humor, Jami gently guides us on a path to heal the wounds of diet culture and body image obsession so that we can live vibrantly—as women who are unconditionally loved. Every woman who's ever stressed over the scale or mirror should read this book."

–Heather Creekmore, author of *Compared to Who?*
A Proven Path to Improve Your Body Image and *The Burden of Better*

"This book couldn't have come at a better time—reading it was like rehashing the years of conversations I used to have with my best friend of 17 years about body image and overall unworthiness. Sadly, my best friend passed away after an 8-month battle with endometrial cancer, and as much as I wish I could've given her a copy of this book while she was alive, I'm so thankful it will now be in the hands of women the world over who are dealing with the same issues she did. The battle for a healthy mindset and body image is a war that many of us will endure our entire lifetimes, but it doesn't have to be this way. Jami does an incredible job with her wit and humor to share stories of how she overcame this war herself with the help of Jesus Christ. If you're ready to truly win the battle over your size and caloric intake and to walk in freedom daily, find a comfy spot with a journal and pen in hand and get ready to be challenged."

–Enid Bozic, Founder and podcast host of *Imperishable Beauty*,
adjunct professor of Communications at Vanguard University

"As someone who has struggled with her weight and body image for years, I fell in love with this gentle, loving, and truthful reminder that the Gospel is true for every part of us: heart, soul, mind, and body. Jami makes you feel as if you'd pulled up a chair at her kitchen table while she shares God-centered, Gospel-filled, Bible-based truth that your heart and body are desperate to hear. Jami offers you hope and gives you Jesus."

–Jill E. McCormick, co-author of *Sister, Walk in Truth*
and host of the *Grace in Real Life* podcast

Well, Girl

An
Inside-Out
Journey to
Wellness

Jami Amerine

SHILOH RUN  PRESS
An Imprint of Barbour Publishing, Inc.

For Frannie

Contents

Foreword 9

Introduction. 11

Part One: Under My Skin 17

Chapter One: Come Monday 19

Chapter Two: In His Image. 39

Chapter Three: Stone-Cold Saved 55

Chapter Four: Woman 71

Chapter Five: How to Make Apple Pie. 89

Chapter Six: Create in Me 101

Chapter Seven: Cha-ching! 119

Chapter Eight: Tick-tock 135

Part Two: Full Frontal Freedom. 149

Chapter Nine: The Ax Murderer's Diet 151

Chapter Ten: Plan A 163

Chapter Eleven: The Weigh-In 175

Chapter Twelve: Believe Beloved 189

Chapter Thirteen: Taste and See Wisdom 201

Chapter Fourteen: Sacred Sweat (Don't Panic) . . . 213

Chapter Fifteen: The Making of a Princess. 227

Conclusion 249

Acknowledgments 253

"Should you shield the canyons from the windstorms, you would never see the true beauty of their carvings."
Elisabeth Kübler-Ross

Foreword

*A*s I write these words, it's just a few days after Thanksgiving. We traveled to Kansas to visit our extended family for the holiday, and I noticed something interesting about the large gym at the hotel where we stayed for the week.

I went down to walk on the treadmill every morning during the week of Thanksgiving. Most mornings, the gym was completely empty and I had it all to myself.

But not on Thanksgiving morning. Nope. The gym was packed. It was loud. It was busy. And I could barely find a treadmill that wasn't being used.

Now, it may have been that there were just more people staying there that morning, which meant more foot traffic in the gym. However, I don't think that was all there was to it. I also have a sneaking suspicion that all those guests were using the gym in an attempt to justify the calories they'd be eating later that day—Thanksgiving meals.

Isn't that the message we are bombarded with every day? That we need to earn the calories we eat or punish ourselves with eating little and exercising more when we binge on a bag of Doritos?

The magazines at the grocery checkout lane boast headlines like "How to drop 10 pounds in a week!" The TV commercials promise easy and almost instantaneous weight loss if we just try this new diet or drink these miracle shakes.

We think that losing weight, fitting into a smaller dress size, or being able to zip up our pre-pregnancy jeans is what is going to make us happy, loved, and valuable.

But I'm here to tell you that being a size 2 is not what will solve your insecurities. You are already loved and valuable—no matter your size. But until you begin to believe that, no amount of weight loss or dieting will ever be enough.

In *Well, Girl: An Inside-Out Journey to Wellness*, Jami invites you to join her on a vulnerable journey to stop dieting and start living as loved. She candidly shares her struggles, mistakes, and successes and encourages you to find your wholeness in Jesus, not the latest fad eating plan.

If you've ever beaten yourself up for the number on the scale or battled feelings of insecurity because of your size, you need to read this book. It's a fresh approach to an age-old conflict, and it's not like any wellness plan, weight loss manual, or healthy eating book you've read before. . .and it just might be the last one you'll ever need to read!

Crystal Paine
November 2019

Introduction

"You know, God hasn't ever asked me to write something without allowing me to walk through it first."

My wise and all-knowing author friend chimed this, wagging a finger at me, half with a warning and half wink-wink-nudge-nudge.

Friend, I've been walking this out for thirty-two of my forty-eight years.

I have tenure.

This is the role (not to be confused with *roll*) of my lifetime.

It is ironic; as I sit down to start this book, it is my anniversary. Five years ago, on this very day, I started my blog. And now, I sit here staring at my computer screen, knowing book three will be. . .*hard.*

I was forced into blogging. Two seasoned authors at a writers' conference wouldn't let me out of the room until I opened an account. Also, they believed it was time to buy a computer. I opened my Word-Press account on my iPhone. And then I sat down and flippantly made categories. In the back of my mind, I heard the voice, you know the one. . .*the One.*

Body image.

No.

Yes.

No.

Yes.

No way.

Jami, baby. . .*yes.*

And my heart broke one thousand times over because He knew I knew that this is the equivalent of my posting nude pictures of myself. I was primed and ready—seriously, I even got a spray tan. I was going to do nudies instead of this book. And I think I could have been convinced. But my husband and publisher would not sign off on a centerfold. So instead, this is me in my rawest form.

Fully clothed, completely exposed.

I do not come to you a size 4. That would be cheesy and cliché. But when I finish this, and you close this book, you will know how far we have come.

And I fully believe we will never be the same.

There are some things I'd like to tell you. A few of them, things I believe will change you forever. Not because of me, but because of who you are in Jesus. As I prepare to go into the deep, I am broken and delighted. I needed this freedom, and I needed to say it out loud. I need to know why, *why* has it taken this long? Why has it been so hard? And why is this the language of so many Christian women? "*If only I looked better, then. . .*"

I have read many a self-help, body-image, diet, fitness, and wellness book. Perhaps I have read them all. I suspect the difference between those books and this one is

1. Most of the authors pen their advice from a place of recovered, thin, well, and perfected. I am starting here, unraveling with you.

2. None of them ever seem to consider the whole female being. The parts of a woman that want to be well and loved for who she is—and carrot sticks and five more laps around the block don't seem to address what is really missing. Key factors that have been neglected, stifled, or seemingly destroyed. . .yet, they are there, waiting to be restored, embellished, and perfected. This is why the first section of this book is about the heart of the woman and not her pants size. I am convinced the inside will free the outside.

3. This book is for every woman. Fat, thin, tall, short, *all* women. Because this book is about the struggle we all face as seekers of Christ, and what I now know has been the greatest barrier to true freedom.

4. I, the author of this book, am not the answer. I am not here to convince you to follow me off a cliff or eat what I eat or work out like I work out. And while I am not the answer, I know Who is. And I am certain He alone can set us free and end the madness that is the pursuit of confidence, health, and the pursuit of wellness.

Please know this isn't a fad diet or "eating plan." This is the place where I surrender a lifelong struggle and invite God to show me the next right thing. It is humiliating and liberating. An author sitting behind a crystal glass of whiskey is romanticized by the drink, simultaneously lamenting and applauding it for aiding him in the mastery of words. Should the vice be cocaine or vodka, God knows you would champion my struggle; give glory to the Maker and His aid in my recovery.

"Glory to God! She's off the sauce!"

Alas, that is not my vice. Well, sauce, yes. Alfredo sauce to be specific. With garlic bread. Also, Italian cream cake for dessert. And alcoholism is no joking matter, nor is drug addiction. But honestly, they get a lot more respect than food addiction, low self-worth, and a big butt. No, chubby is not cool. And yeah, I will kick you in the teeth if you chime in, "But you have such a pretty face!" Heaven help. I am not a violent person, but don't test me.

Let me start with this reminder to you: it's not what goes into a girl that makes her unclean, it's what comes out. And that thing, the thing where someone compliments with a "but" is not a compliment. It is a passive-aggressive attempt to criticize.

Boom.

Let's get that straight right now. There is no "but" in a decent apology. A good "I love you" with a "but" in it bears the mark of a contingent love.

This was brought to my attention around about

the eighth time I became negatively conscious of my body. A boy that I was dating in high school said it. He was a lifeguard at the local pool. I was fifteen years old, a size zero, nearly five feet nine inches. He came down from his stand to eat lunch with me—a lunch I packed for him. I had on a turquoise bikini with a ruffle across my impossibly tiny bust and a coinciding ruffle on the bum. A bum you could get three bounces off a quarter on.

I'm glad I don't have a physical picture of that day. I might need to be admitted to a psych ward if I had an actual visual of how itty-bitty I was. The boyfriend was tan, tall, and blond, and he approached me with a scowl. He pointed at my tummy and said, "I am sorry, *but* you are getting too fat to wear a bikini. I love you, *but* don't come back up here in a swimsuit until you have done a sit-up or five thousand. It's embarrassing."

And so it began.

Now here I am, thirty-five years later, a lot larger than that sunny July afternoon. And I know, I know what you are thinking. *"If only you could go back and tell that girl. . ."*

You know what? No. There is no *but*. I am sorry that happened. I wish I could say I love the way I look at forty-eight and that I have complete peace with who I am. But that is why I am here. If any other thing in the world had gone on, I wouldn't be here now, staring freedom in the face and sharing it with you, my friend.

The trick, the rabbit up my sleeve that brought me to this place of composition, is worth it. No friend, really, it is. For if we do not stumble, struggle, and fall on our faces, we never look up and cry, "Father, help me." And I propose, He is the only answer. A divided heart, whether you realize it yet or not, that is the stumbling block. In my darkest hours, my Jesus is the light. So I'd rather have fallen to my knees so that He alone can help me up and create something entirely new. The guide to knowing Him starts with needing Him. And oh, goodness, I do. I do need this, God. I need Him to fill in my gaps, help me up off the floor, and guide me in ways of wisdom. This struggle is worth it. Draw me gently to my knees, my Adonai.

It is here, facedown, out of ideas, I write these words and call out:

Are you there, God? It's me, Jami with no e . . .
Yes. I will do this hard thing. I will tell all. I will
bare all. . .because of You. I trust You. I believe
You. I know You know the answer to the dilemma
every daughter who picks up this book faces in
the pursuit of peace. My answer is yes,
no but.

> *Yes.*
> *Here I am, send me. . . .*
> *Results this time totally typical—typical,*
> *that is, for His Beloved.*

Love, Jami

Part One

Under My Skin

Therefore, with minds that are alert and fully sober,
set your hope on the grace to be brought to you
when Jesus Christ is revealed at his coming.

1 Peter 1:13

CHAPTER ONE

Come Monday

"Before I formed you in the womb I knew you,
before you were born I set you apart."
JEREMIAH 1:5

*N*ever would I believe I would meet you here. Me, Jami Amerine, lover of all things shiny. Girly girl among the fanciful pretty, and. . .perfect. I love lipstick, lashes, blushes, powders, perfumes, and all things lovely. *Who am I?* was all I could muster as I looked down at an impossible number. . .seventy pounds more than I could fathom. This battle has raged on for far too long. And truth be told, eighty pounds ago, I believed I was obese. I wasn't even phased to learn I fell into this category now, because I believed myself to be so since I was ten.

Oh, whatever, judge all you'd like. Don't you recall the first time you questioned the lumps on your thighs? The bump on your tummy? Even at my fittest, on the way to run a half-marathon, I cried all the way to the event. Fully consumed with my pre-race weight. After the race? I didn't eat for two days, copiously consumed with stepping on the scales and seeing the number I loved more than any number on the planet. Alas, finally, I caved and ate. . .and ate and ate and ate.

Condemnation rattles in my ears: "Too much, too gross, too fat, too heavy, too. . .pathetic." Perhaps I would not want to discuss these things with you had I not finally been set free; and no, I am not a size 4, that would be so banal of me. I propose, my vulnerability is less than darling and more a desperate plea for someone to step forward and yelp, "ME TOO!!!" Granted, I have written enough to know you are out there. . .whimpering, *"Me too."*

Hello, friend. Welcome. I have so much to tell you. So much to promise. Pull up a chair. I will grab another cup and tell you things. . .things you must know, stuff I wish didn't have to be said, and most certainly the story of my freedom and success. However, this is not your average eat more lettuce and do your cardio wellness book. This is a total freedom, "we are finally done with this nonsense," wellness book. In the first section, we are going to identify and slay the things that keep us stuck in the cycle of "trying and trying again." And then, in the second section, we are moving on for good.

A Fat Girl's Guide to Jesus

I guess this book started amid a near-death experience. For the better part of two weeks, we had been battling a nasty stomach bug. As far as viruses go, it was a disease of peculiar symptoms. Body aches, chills, fever, headache, nausea, and unconsciousness. Yeah, unconsciousness was the good part; actually, it was a nightmare until my husband, Justin, got home to monitor our then-four- and six-year-old sons, whom we lovingly refer to as "the Vandals," Sam and Charlie. In my deathbed state, I could hear the little boys laughing, and I could smell peanut butter, but I couldn't do anything about it. Had the persistent scent been kerosene, I still would have been paralyzed to react.

I know it wasn't a hallucination because my briefcase still had traces and there was a note on the fridge that said Buy Peanut Butter. I asked Justin about it, and he just held up his hand and said, "I don't want to talk about it." As I stretched and twisted the kinks out of my over-rested body, I spied my *new* list for the week. This list was started on Monday. They all start on Monday for me.

> 1. Get up at 4 a.m. and spend quiet time with Jesus.
> 2. Walk 10,000 steps.
> 3. Eat clean.
> 4. Teach Sam to read.

This time, I made it two days.

> 1. I did talk to Jesus. I asked Him to end my suffering and welcome me home. But I don't know what time it was.
> 2. My step counter showed an image of a tombstone and a daisy. It suspects I died.
> 3. Saltines and Gatorade. . .ugh, I can't.
> 4. Who is Sam?

This is where the heavy work of hating me always seems to land. *I'll have to make a new list because I am a failure.* You know where I'm coming from, right? Whatever the list, we good Christian girls have been taught that all things get fixed when we perfect our walk with Jesus, wash our face, and try harder. First on our to-do list of getting it all right: get right with God. In our finest, most determined penmanship we write:

1. Get closer to Jesus.

And I have been a size 4, and I have been a size 16, and it was only recently a friend said to me, "You really believe that God loves you more or less because of the size of your jeans?"

Yes, that is correct. What don't you understand about this?

Well, this was the thinking keeping me stuck. Does this sound familiar? Every diet or exercise regime I have ever started began with:

1. Get up early for quiet time alone with the Lord.

Then, every time I slept past my alarm, even if I had been up all night with the sick kids, I would throw in the towel, give in and give up, and eat Frosted Flakes and Pop-Tarts for breakfast. I would skip Pilates and give up all hope of bodily perfection, repent (obnoxiously), dine on my feelings, and promise to start over. . .come Monday.

Come Monday, everything will be better. Come

Monday, it is all Jesus all the time. I will be the best Jami I can be—next week. I would use the rest of that redemptive week to get all the crap out of my system; that is, add crap to my system that the new-found relationship I will pursue with Jesus next week won't permit.

Next week, Jesus and I will be unstoppable. These kinds of deals, with myself or God, set me up for failure, again keeping me stuck. This week, I will eat Cheetos and watch reruns of *Friends*. During the commercials, I will write down my new goals in my brand-new "All things work together for good. . ." journal with a purple pen. Purple for royalty be-cause I will be a princess, daughter of the King, *come Monday.*

Consider this: Is there any other relationship in your life you give up on Wednesdays at noon with the promise to try that relationship again on Monday? Is there a single person in your life whom you would feed garbage to, call names, and abuse in the hopes of treating that person any better next week?

So, as I clicked on the link to open my new head-shots for my book publisher, I did so with one eye closed, terrified at what I might see. Horrified that God was about to pull the rug out and go, *"JUST KID-DING. YOU'RE TOO FAT TO WRITE A BOOK ABOUT ME!"* I prayed, "Please let there be just one good one, and then starting Monday, I am never eating sugar or refined carbs again!"

What was the last deal you made with God? We

may have every good intention to meet Him in the middle. But friend, it's a setup for guilt and shame. Every time.

But as the pictures loaded, I had a life-altering moment: *If Christ dwells in me, how am I able to reasonably distinguish "starting over"?* If I am the temple and He has promised never to leave or forsake me, what could possibly be so awful about me? What is too much? Moreover, what is not enough?

One by one, the pictures loaded. Tears filled my eyes, and my heart began to pound. I know this girl. I know those curves. I recognized the laugh lines, the smirk. And I knew, while there were a few age spots and some teeth whitening to do; I am no Cindy Crawford, but I am Jami. No *e*. And I know me. I am a daughter of the Most High, and He knows me and still died so that I could be free.

God chose the perfect Lamb. Grace is the eternal remnant of that sacrifice. Eternity is the reward; but I am confident that until we get there, He has more for us here than we have tapped into. He will move how He moves and save how He saves. We may not understand why He does things, how He makes all things new; but this much I know for sure: I don't have to wait until Monday to ask.

Certainly, this is a great folly among humans and our God. That we can put Him on hold while we. . .sin? Is that the goal? "Well, I messed up again. I guess I will keep messing up and then next week I will do better."

Press PAUSE.

Okay, let's look at that from the view of marriage. If I were caught in the act of adultery, what would Justin's reaction be to me saying, "Well, darn babe. Gig's up. You caught me. Since you caught me midweek, I am going to finish prowling the streets and hooking up with strangers through the weekend. I will get back to you on Monday. . .and then I will never do it again, I promise."

Justin is an easygoing guy, but I can assure you, he would not be cool with this. It is a nod to exactly how patient God really is; because how many times have I "started over" in my salvation walk? How many times were we encouraged to start over? How many times have we recounted our sins, folly, and shortcomings and begged to be different? This is the quicksand I have spent the majority of my life in. This is the sticky place the enemy wants to keep me. Starting over and over, believing that I am never "getting it." Or worse, that the main objective of my life is to finally be the ideal weight so I can have a good relationship with God.

The word *confession* in its original Greek form was *homologeo*, and it means "to agree with, to speak the same thing, to celebrate, worship, profess, acknowledge."

So, were a girl to significantly and accurately confess in the language of the New Testament to God, one would have to be in alignment with Him about what He says about me.

Redeemed. Amen.

Whole. Amen.

Forgiven. Yes!

Saved. You betcha.

But the lingo many of us are taught is all about the sinner.

Stop sinning.

No, really, stop it. And we sign up for the next big study or the women's retreat in four months; and then, yes, on that day, we will finally get it. I believe the plan-ahead mentality of perfection is a grand tactic the enemy uses in the church to perpetuate sinful behavior and keep us separated from the God of our creation and redemption. What a tragedy this is. If we are always waiting and planning, we aren't tapping into God. It always keeps us at arm's-length from Him. Waiting keeps us stuck. This is why we are still here.

Years ago, I attended a confession-based women's retreat. I knew we were doing all the "confess and repent" things. We spent an hour listing all our sins, and then we burned them. Then we went and listed some more and burned them, and then we did it again, and then we all got "re-baptized." The problem with this type of exercise is it is exponentially anti-Gospel. And I confess, before going, I went on a four-day "binge" of sorts. I went to all my favorite restaurants, maxed out three credit cards on clothes for the three-day retreat, and watched two movies—icky movies that I normally wouldn't watch.

In my mind, I had decided to get all the "sinning"

out of my system, keep God at bay, and deal with Him and His lofty commands at the retreat. I decidedly went and did what I wanted and, without actually saying it, was intentionally communicating, *Lord, I am doing what I want. I will be perfect next week. Please leave me alone.* The "come Monday" mentality perpetuates the lie that we must live at arm's-length with this amazing God until we get it right. How do you keep God at arm's-length in your life? It may look different than mine, but I propose we all do it.

Essentially I made up a laundry list of what I saw as good and bad. I gorged myself under the "tree of good and evil." Meaning, I believed I could be bad and then say "sorry" and be good. In doing all the "work" to obtain forgiveness, I deemed myself righteous by said works, wholly neglecting any form of humility and putting more stock in my ability to save myself. Which, for the record, I cannot do. And neither can you. Next, whether I knew it or not at the time, I was encouraging the pleasure of rebellion, with the false reality that I didn't really have to be different to be more of a "Jesus-girl." I could just go through the "works" of the cleansing retreat again next year. Where, by the way, I got to hang out with friends, did not have to cook or clean, and had some time away from my kids. *Party.* This is where we get our hearts and our faith mixed up. Here is why we struggle to follow the rules. Here is where we sometimes use the Word of God against us. . .rather than as a gift for us. It occurs to me as I am typing this: Does it even say a word about the sin of obesity, thinness, lack of exercise, or bikini-ready body in the Bible? Stay with me, because yes, there are references to wellness, gluttony, and the temple; but under what law are we bound to be 100 percent healthy, or we are sinning?

> *Their destiny is destruction, their god is their stomach, and their glory is in their shame. Their mind is set on earthly things.* (Philippians 3:19)

> *When you sit to dine with a ruler, note well what is before you, and put a knife to your throat if you are given to gluttony. Do not crave his delicacies, for that food is deceptive.* (Proverbs 23:1–3)

Additionally, if we fall ill, is that a sin? Or a punishment? Because I know some good and decent humans who have cancer. Under the Hebrew law, there were 613 commandments, all of which no one was capable of keeping. Under the Mosaic covenant, it was slimmed down to 10. And we dine at the smorgasbord of law, counting ourselves well because we are or aren't doing a few of them?

How do we pick? I propose this is another of the biggest detriments to our walk with a good and loving God. We are staying stuck by

    1.   confusing covenants and mixing up the law; and

2. adding to the completed work of the cross and bathing in contempt—contempt He doesn't have for us, His darlings.

Under the New Covenant, made between God and Himself, we do not live under the law. We live under grace, and it is written on our hearts. Legalism is what keeps us HERE. We're too busy beating ourselves up about messing up rather than living in grace. People who feel like failures stay stuck. If success breeds success, then what comes from failure?

Galatians 5:1 says, "It is for freedom that Christ has set us free. Stand firm, then, and do not let yourselves be burdened again by a yoke of slavery." And honestly, friend, I don't want to go back. Chances are, you don't either. Let's decide we won't entertain the belief we must do anything to earn God's love. The freedom of grace is a life free of guilt and condemnation; you are free to walk away from the law because you believe.

Yes, we can do all the things and make up some new ones, fully believing we are righteous by how good we are and fully buying into "I'll try again Monday!" Or we can accept the gift of baptism and salvation and be led by the Spirit and never have to hide in shame again.

In our society, good equals reward and bad equals punishment. If I obey traffic laws, my insurance rates are modest and I am free from traffic fines and accidents. If I text and drive, speed through school zones, or drive under the influence, I could lose my license, harm myself and/or others, and land in jail. One plus one equals two.

And in our minds, this is an excellent way to navigate life, a life under a law written in stone. In an effort to secure hell-fire insurance, we say yes to Jesus, and we are "saved." Our salvation means that we will go to heaven. Bonus. *But*, and there's that word, *but*. But now, we must do better. We must be better, and we must work hard—or else. And the "or else" is easily argued depending on the denomination. There is the "once saved always saved" crowd, then there's the "use it or lose it" crowd, and then there are a few others that make up some stuff according to the gravity of the sin. The sin that was overcome on the cross. *But* that is hardly the point.

Right.

So, who was the first authority who said, "Too many pounds or too few pounds are a sin against the Lord. You need to be perfect."

Okay, well, I want to be perfect! But, um, what is perfect?

Is there a BMI scale in the Bible? Did Jesus know how much He weighed? And was His weight perfectly proportional to His height?

Another way we stay stuck is social media. A tool of the enemy that gives us visual depictions of what we are not. A little tidbit of what we used to be. A few days ago, I got one of those Facebook notices, which should really come with a warning: Five years ago today, you looked this smokin' hot, or five years ago today, your out-of-control teen was this cute. Please click now if you are prepared to have your heart squeezed like a boob in a mammogram device.

Click.

My notification was a picture of me after running my second half-marathon. I am just not a tiny person. Nearly five-nine, busty, big hair, big teeth, big feet, they are Nordic features indicative of childrearing and village pillaging. Yet the picture slew me for two reasons: (1) I was about seventy pounds thinner then, and (2) because I remember that morning very well.

I was utterly disgusted with myself.

I cried all the way to the race to meet my running partner. I prayed out loud that *come Monday* I would be better. Monday, I would get up at 4:30. I would only eat raw vegan. I would add back the four cycling classes I had neglected this training season. And I would fast on Tuesdays and Thursdays. Mind you, back then, my fasts were more like hunger strikes rather than loving sacrifices or offerings for clarity.

A week and a half later, I tore my calf muscle and my plantar fasciitis teaching a kickboxing class, one I had no business teaching. A year later, I was forty pounds heavier and hobbled. And I told people, "God was teaching me something." And I set my alarm for 4 a.m. I failed repeatedly and counted myself fatter, sadder, and further from God.

If only I were a size 2, God's favor would rest upon me. Things would be better for my family. If only I were physically perfect and had my act together, things would flow, and God would be pleased with me.

Lies.

Lies that kept me stuck. Unrealistic expectations of God, me, and others. Do you hear them too? Yeah, I thought so. The lies of the enemy plague women of every shape, size, height, and weight. Now, with yet another thirty pounds plaguing me, and with four years of writing professionally under my very tight belt, I have even more proof that this is one of the enemy's primary talents. The resounding gong? Women who continue to say how hard they are "trying. . ." and still, things aren't better.

Dear sister, *things are fabulous.*

Yes, your marriage, body, kids, household, job, or whatever might be in shambles—there is no better time or pants size than right now to believe in your birthright: *Daughter.*

Christ died for me while I was still a sinner. And the blood worked. Meaning, the sacrifice of the blood of Jesus accomplished the cleansing of sin, *once and for all. This is WHY we can move forward into a healthier view of ourselves and healthier choices. This is the antidote for our worthless feelings.*

He, in all His goodness, is not more or less pleased with me when I am rocking a foster baby, delivering meals to shut-ins, or having a second or uh. . .third lemon-filled pastry. How good is this God? He knew I couldn't, so He did. And then He invited me to a banquet to indulge in His goodness. No go-betweens, no wise savants. He wants to be with me. Just as I am.

Beloved Living

Now, let me be clear. This is going to be a little more complex than I am about to offer, but I am going to let you cheat a little. Among the many books I have read trying to fix all that is wrong with me, one thing I hate is not knowing how to make at least some of the change, *NOW*! For the purposes of this book, we are calling it the Goal of Beloved Living. And the Goal of Beloved Living is threefold:

1. Seek Him in all things. And this is going to be HUGE, so keep reading.
2. Discern what we think, what we believe about ourselves, God, and the factors that influence those beliefs.
3. Make genuine peace with yourself by accepting the truth of who you are in Jesus. Again, that might mean mentally or physically, spiritually, or all the above. I believe in doing so, we will have our eyes open to an abundance of peace that He fully intended us to embrace. And yes, there are health benefits that will follow.

Spoiler alert: I am healthier and happier than I have ever been. How can that be? I am not crash-dieting, overexercising, or bullying myself into food submission—these things on the long list of ways we sabotage ourselves from finding the courage to take a step toward living healthier. Nope, I am just "doing" Plan A.

For now, if you want to practice what I call "Plan A," these are the principles. These will challenge you to step over all the reasons you're stuck, but they are small steps that have brought me real freedom.

1. *You can eat anything you want; you can exercise as little or as much as you like.* There is no condemnation in Christ. All things are permissible. All I want you to consider is this: *Is it beneficial?* That is the mindset I want you to focus on. The concept is derived from 1 Corinthians 10:23, that everything is permissible, but not everything is beneficial. If you are currently following an eating plan, okay, that is fine. All I ask is that before you eat anything, you get in the habit of saying these words, "All is permissible; is it beneficial?"

2. *Taste your food.* This may seem like common sense, but I propose we, especially those of us who are steeped in a "tree of good and evil" eating mentality, that indulge like crazy people, do not truly taste our food. Which brings me to three.

3. *Feast with the Father.* And maybe this should be number one. But I wanted to list it last because, when you are feasting with the Father, I want you to come to Him and give thanks for whatever is before you. Then, I hope to instill in us a standard by which we seek Him first.

"Hey, Jesus, I want this. I know I can have it, but is it truly for me?" Take a beat and really focus in on what He is telling you. Remember, He is a gentleman. If you hear the words, "NO! YOU COW! YOU CAN'T HAVE THAT UNLESS YOU WANT TO BE BURIED IN A PIANO BOX!" That is not Jesus. So lean into the blessing of taste. Smell your food. Let it melt. Note the texture, taste, and temperature. Invite Him to eat with you. Not just a rote nod to the cheeseburger. . .an opportunity to experience Him and the good food He has provided.

Don't worry, I will be developing this more in-depth in a bit as it pertains to how dearly you are loved. For now, I want you to try this method of choice. *Hey, Jesus, I know I can have that or do that, but is it of benefit?*

This is your assignment: As you read and go about your day, just ask yourself and Jesus, "How is this of benefit to me?" And here is the thing, after you establish if it is or isn't of benefit, if you still want to do it, do it. I want us to take the shackles off and taste freedom. I promise, the pendulum will balance; for now, you are free from the law of good and bad.

Dear Eve

I can empathize with Eve. Do not cross this line, and in my stubborn flesh, I am just going to have to. The consequences? Hiding in the bushes, trying to cover up that which is "bad." And the question comes, "Who told you that you were naked?" (Genesis 3:11). Who first insinuated that there was a problem? That something needed to be different? A shortcut or a new and improved way of doing things.

Here among the living, we turn our noses up at Eve as if she alone had caused this fall. But Eve is me. She is me, and I am her. Under the same circumstances, I too would and have failed the test of "anything but that. . ." Chances are you would have too.

And I hide in shame. Shame is going to be an issue we will address repeatedly. Again, shame is a silent dream killer, and left undetected or dealt with, you will forever stay HERE.

I believe it is possible to walk in the freedom Christ died for and never face shame again. Why? Because God said it was possible. And I believe Him. I believe Paul, whose eyes were open to the truth, and I know God wants freedom for me and you.

May the God of hope fill you with all joy and peace as you trust in him, so that you may overflow with hope by the power of the Holy Spirit. (Romans 15:13)

For the better part of my Christian walk, I have spouted off truths from the Word, never truly believing any of them, scriptures like:

For I am convinced that neither death nor life, neither angels nor demons, neither the present nor the future, nor any powers, neither height nor depth, nor anything else in all creation, will be able to separate us from the love of God that is in Christ Jesus our Lord. (Romans 8:38–39)

This verse was paramount in my faulty beliefs. NOTHING can separate me from the love of Jesus. *But* in my mind, there was a list of things that did. And this is laughable, but it is also very arrogant and terribly sad. I confess I have low self-esteem, except for events surrounding the God of all. I have fully believed I, Jami Jo Amerine, from West Texas, would be His last straw.

I know, there's a wealth of evil going on in the world, but I clung to the belief that if I went over my Weight Watchers points or had a whole calorie Coke, He was moments away from striking me dead with a bolt of lightning. Or worse, punishing me by making one of my kids sick, or dead.

There are parts of that that are funny, but truly, it was a tragic existence.

And oh, friend, I have learned something revolutionary about life and a life cloaked in shame. It will turn your beliefs about yourself upside down. Let us go on this journey together; freedom and peace are just around the corner. Let's not wait until Monday.

Well, Girl Wisdom

We don't have to start over in our relationship with Christ. He is always available. In a healthy relationship, we don't run and hide when we mess up or hit a bump in the road. Moreover, we don't wait until a marked day (say Monday) to get it right. As Christians, aren't we trying to know God better? Have you put Him on "hold"? Can you imagine if one of your children or someone you loved did this? What would you say to them? Could that loved one come to you with anything? Are you ready to start Beloved Living?

Freedom Gain

In the coming chapters, we will talk more about gaining instead of losing. But I want to invite you to write out your thoughts, maybe even a prayer. Have you pushed God aside to "get right" so you can experience Him? Take a few moments to write out what you took away from this chapter. Are you scared to let go of food plans? Talk to Jesus. Perfect love casts out all fear. And whether you have experienced loving God perfectly is irrelevant. He loves you perfectly, and we are about to fall headlong into His arms.

CHAPTER TWO

In His Image

*Do you not know that your bodies are temples of the
Holy Spirit, who is in you, whom you have received
from God? You are not your own; you were bought
at a price. Therefore honor God with your bodies.*
1 CORINTHIANS 6:19–20

Recently a note was sent home from school with our young son, Charlie. The note was directed at our older son, Luke, who is fifteen years Charlie's senior. The note read:

> Dear Mr. and Mrs. Amerine, could you please
> ask Luke to stop telling Charlie about the dan-
> gers of plastics and the inhumane treatment of
> corporate farming? We cannot make modifi-
> cations to our lunch programs based on these
> teachings, and they are causing Charlie and his
> classmates great stress.

Luke, also known around here as the hippie-baby, is a yoga instructor, a student of holistic medicine, and a champion of sea turtles. Of late, at our favorite Mexican restaurant, he and Charlie gathered all the straws off the table and delivered them to management. Luke said, "Our lunch was fantastic, so was the service. Can I make a suggestion? There were fifteen of us at lunch. Your staff served all our drinks with straws. You could go a long way in discouraging waste and harming wildlife if you would only provide straws when a customer requests one." The manager answered, "I hadn't ever thought of that." The next time we went to eat at the restaurant, the menu read, "We provide straws only to customers who request them."

And we are cognizant of the effect of plastics on our health and planet. We also try and buy humanely cultured, grass-fed or wild-caught meats and fish. And we do this for a variety of reasons, reasons that apply to our lives. But we were faced with a question: Do we tell Charlie he isn't allowed to speak his convictions? No, we can't expect the school to buy humanitarianly harvested chicken nuggets; but yep, I want my children to recognize their bodies as temples and the earth as their charge. And upon further investigation, that was Charlie's basic answer, "I just said, 'Ims not gonna eat dose nuggets 'cause Lukey didn't know if the chickens gots to play outside or lived therms whole life in a stinky cage. I want to eat food that got to play fair.' " Reasonable. So we started packing his lunch.

And Charlie is young…well, so is Luke. But I admire this conviction, caring about not just the outer but the insides. The hope that the food you ate wasn't in a stinky cage. Making efforts to protect God's world from things that never erode and destroy His creatures. Furthermore, there is that image, the stinky cage. No freedom, no peace, no green grass. And I am convicted and hopeful; I will be more alert, privy to that which robs life, both physically and mentally.

Friend, chew on this: Do you know your body is a temple? When we don't understand the power of our creation, we don't understand the relevance of taking care of ourselves. Do I have any idea of the precision of my creation? Can I process what it means if just my family cuts back on the use of plastics? And have I given any thought to where my food comes from? Do I consider myself important enough? Do I love myself enough to care about every single aspect of my Beloved Living? Remember, Beloved Living is to

1. Seek Him in all things.
2. Discern what we think, what we believe about ourselves, God, and the factors that influence those beliefs.
3. Make genuine peace with yourself by accepting the truth of who you are in Jesus.

But it was this thought process that led to another memory. An image flashed in my mind of a recent encounter at a speaking engagement. Before the program started, I stood backstage, going over my notes. I looked up and noticed a woman, maybe thirty years old, holding a copy of my first book, waiting to talk to me. She was a tiny thing, not quite five feet tall. She had huge blue eyes, creamy rose-hued skin, and thin, long blond hair to her waist. She was as wide as she was tall through her bust, but I noted she probably had on size 2 jeans. Her pink blouse bulged across her heavy bosom, a single button hanging on for dear life. I smiled and said, "Hello." And she advanced toward me with her hand outstretched.

As my huge hand enveloped hers, I noted she was as dainty as a toddler. Her fingers cool, smooth, and tiny. As our eyes connected, I was stunned by her natural beauty. Her voice was high pitched with a twang of a southern drawl that was both charming and adorable. She asked me to sign her copy of my book and gushed over the meeting. As we talked, she tugged at her blouse, fidgeted with her buttons, trying to stay focused on the conversation.

But I knew. She was consumed with worry over her appearance, and I, mine. From far away, I imagine one might have labeled her obese. I doubt she weighed more than a hundred pounds. However, her disproportionate breasts alluded to a heavier build. She was darling, altogether kind, and precious. We talked for about ten minutes, and when I bent down to hug her, I felt the self-consciousness of my height, wide shoulders, big hair, and equivalently enormous bosom. I jotted the encounter down in my notes and prayed that I would be able to address it.

Praying.

Waiting.

Because honestly, what's the answer? How do you come to a peaceable meeting with an "awkward" body? Is there a stage or age where a woman can say, "Yep, my waist is eighteen inches, and I wear a 52FF bra, and I am totally cool with this, so I will treat myself with kindness and careful habits"? Where is the verse line and reference for too short, too busty, too thin, too tall, too wide? I fully believe we have been painfully trained by ourselves and the world that our bodies are not normal or beautiful. Ah, yes, here it is. The scripture that is a nod to our perfection:

God created mankind in his own image, in the image of God he created them; male and female he created them. (Genesis 1:27)

I propose this is why we CAN move into healthier living. When we choose to believe this, we will start respecting our bodies out of respect for our Creator.

Okay, I hear you. . .but when He created me in His image, was He aware of the upcoming skinny jean fad? Because, yeah, that is not a look I can pull off. And why are they called skinny jeans even when they are in the Women's World section under 28 PLUS PLUS?

In the quest for perfection, someone tell me, what is perfect?

I noted a morbidly obese woman on a power scooter at Walmart the other day. What caught my eye about her was we had on the same shoes. The shoes are called Reebok Easy Tones. They are an athletic shoe that boasts of an ability to shape your legs into something fantastic. But upright on my Viking-stout, 38-inseam legs, I cannot say I have noticed a difference. And I am hard-pressed to know how they are effective if you aren't walking but are on a power scooter? Still, we all hope, we all cling to the illusion of perfection. We have our credit cards armed and ready to try something, anything, to achieve something. . .*else.*

Yes, something other than what we were dealt with, something that looks more toned, more smooth, more shapely. Like Eve, who told us we were naked. Who first drew our eyes down to look at our belly buttons and begin to pick apart, "What is wrong with me?"

More than likely someone pointed out something to you that defined something in you as "*too—*." A lousy boyfriend, a hateful relative, or perhaps a stranger. But someone, somewhere, first alerted us to something about ourselves that just doesn't sit right. Can you pinpoint the first moment? Well, I submit that self-hatred keeps us focused on self and not on God and all He has planned for us.

As a child, we constantly moved, at least thirteen times before I graduated from high school. Whenever we moved, I struggled to make friends. And the message I received from my parents? "They are just jealous of you because you are too pretty." By most accounts, this comes across as a good problem to have; but as a child, all I knew for certain was that I was lonely and obviously "too" much of something. The bigger confusion was that I was awkward. I was gangly, my hair was ENORMOUS, and my teeth were a hot mess. I was an undiagnosed dyslexic, and my struggles in school left me segregated and labeled a problem.

The confusing message was that I was *too much*, which invoked "jealousy." But at school, I was not enough. Which resulted in isolation and loneliness. Rejection kept me in bondage to fear. Can you identify with that? And while I was blessed with adoring parents, and I know that is not the case for every eye that falls on this page, I have come to believe, beyond the adoration or lack that comes from humans, our God adores. Still, what were or are the scenarios that defined you in your beliefs as *too little* or *too much*?

Besides being "too pretty," I was encouraged to believe that the world somehow revolved around me. I recall the election night in 1976. I had just turned five. Results were running late, my parents had hosted a barbecue, and our extended family had come over to wait and see who the next president would be. Decidedly, the children would not stay up, so my mom fashioned a campout on the floor of the basement and proceeded to tuck myself and a dozen cousins into cushy quilted pallets on the floor.

I inquired, "Mommy, who did you vote for?" She answered, "Well, you shouldn't really ask people who they voted for. It is a personal and important decision. But, just between you and me, I voted for your father."

As my cousins whispered and joked, I sunk into my quilted haven and wept silently. Certainly, if my mom had voted for my dad, everyone else upstairs did too. And this would mean only one thing. My dad was going to be the next president of the United States. We would have to move to Washington, DC, away from our beloved family and friends. Nothing would ever be the same, and I was heartbroken.

Childish? Yes. However, I was just a child. Not only are we created in His image, He also encourages us to remain childlike in our belief. And my parents gushed of my perfection and abilities. And the world was on standby, waiting to prove that belief wrong. In second grade on a bus ride to school, my homework was ridiculed as sloppy and ridiculous. Strange? My dad had said it was perfect. In seventh grade, I wasn't picked for the dance team, but my mom and cousins had assured me I was the best. In ninth grade, in a modeling contest for which I did not make it to the finals, I questioned, *How can that be?* I had always been told I was gorgeous. Not as talented, too much, too little, better than everyone else, but not quite enough, way too. . .

Too.

If only this word could be banned, it would be utterly delightful. In my perfect world, we would just not have *too* or *but*. Perhaps then my daughters and sisters in Christ would have some level of peace with who they are and what makes them incredibly "just right."

Possibly, well definitely, in my parent's folly, they were over the top in their adoration. And maybe your parents lacked any. But I am certain of this: there is a Father who can fill in the gaps of all the past mistakes, whether they be exceedingly gracious or lacking an ounce of an accolade.

In our Americanese way of describing beings, what can set us apart as "just right"? Is there a single way we aren't self-conscious or unhappy with our appearance or performance? I propose the answer is yes. But it takes some work. It takes some digging, some tears, and some resting in the completed work of the cross.

Moment by moment, from one pants size to the next—larger or smaller—the blood worked. Jesus was the perfect sacrifice, and His blood covers a multitude of sins, and love covers the rest. Again, this is WHY we can (and will at some point if we choose) find the confidence and courage to be healthier from the inside out. The dance is ongoing. He is continually kind and merciful and madly in love with you. The essence of Him is enough. Believing Him is outstanding. Only good comes from Him, despite me. He never leaves or forsakes me. And, as I mentioned before, His love never waits until Monday.

So, what is the key to finally looking in the mirror and saying to yourself, *Okay, this is me. This is my current situation. For this moment, I am okay with this. His grace is sufficient. I commit to self-understanding and acceptance as a work in progress. For now, this is good, and I receive the acceptance my God has for me.* I would like to propose it is shame that keeps us in want. I believe ridding ourselves of shame then is key, for it is the cornerstone of our lack of worth and the motivator for our habitual need to "start over." And this, this is huge. *I believe that the enemy uses shame to keep us stuck.*

This is lofty, but how dare we be ashamed of the temple where God has chosen to dwell? My friend and fellow author Carey Scott unearthed shame in an entirely new light when she said, "Guilt is being sorry for something you have done. Shame is being sorry for who you are."

Shame is being sorry for who you are.

And if you are ashamed, I propose you have neglected the truth of exactly who you are. I know this was true of me. I wasn't just guilty of overconsumption and an abnormal affection for soft cheeses, a partiality to napping, and exaggerated breast tissue. I was ashamed of who I was. I was ashamed of who I was when I was a size 4, 6, 8, 10, back to 4, 6, 8, 10, 12, 14. And if I was ashamed of who I was, it wasn't ever going to matter the size of my clothes or my hairstyle or marathon medals or prescription medications. Until I was able to decipher truly, I have guilt (not *but*), *AND* I ceased being ashamed of who I was, there would be no progress. So I wrote it out.

You are the daughter of the Most High. He died for you so that He would be with you for eternity. He did this so you would never face condemnation, ever. You are whole and complete. He wants you to live a life of abundant peace and joy and share it with others, so they too will know of His goodness. This is the Good News.

And then I started saying it out loud. Staring directly at myself in the mirror, I spoke this every day for one month. I have done it ever since. I want this kind of freedom for you too. I want you to know who you are because it's vital to this process. Will you take a moment and write out who you are? You can use mine, tweak mine, or write something new altogether. But write it here, at our starting place.

_____

_____

_____

_____

_____

_____

It all comes down to this, the reason we stay stuck. Ready to start living? Sister, it is time to dig deep into the truth of our identity in Jesus Christ. Okay. Sounds like a plan. Any suggestions?

Why yes! And I am so glad you asked! The first is to look at the green grass! This is my favorite metaphor for a life that is sin-focused versus life in grace. And it is simple: if you are focused on sin and what *not to do*, you aren't focused on Jesus. If you are digging at your belly button, picking out all the shame of who you think you are and who you think you "should" be, you never look up at the One who died to set you free.

I liken it to Alcoholics Anonymous. When you go to an AA meeting, they don't do wine tasting and discuss recipes for "light" margaritas; they talk about the freedom they have found away from the drink.

So instead of talking about how to love a disproportionate figure, a bald spot, a lazy eye, or missing limb, let's focus on the freedom of knowing we are loved right now, right here. And yes, there is going to be room for healthy change; but first, let's shift our focus.

Imagine you are trying to teach a toddler to stay out of the street. The street is busy, big trucks come flying past, and there is a high school two blocks up, so teen drivers frequent this street. You warn, "STAY OUT OF THE STREET!" And you say this until you are blue in the face. "STAY OUT OF THE STREET!" Fear of your little one being squashed is the motivation behind this teaching. And love protects. The teaching is genuine in its motive. STAY OUT OF THE STREET. Meanwhile, that street is all you talk about. Your toddler becomes obsessed with what they cannot have.

STAY OUT OF THE STREET.

But now, let's look at the message of the street under the umbrella of everything is permissible, but is it beneficial? You could go into the street, where it is my fear you could be horribly injured or killed. However, here in the green grass, there is a swing set, a Hula-Hoop, there are bubbles and sidewalk chalk. There is a little picnic table with chilled juice boxes, crispy green grapes, cool watermelon, and Goldfish crackers. Here in the green grass, there is a jump rope, a Slip 'N Slide, and a big blue cooler filled with brightly colored Popsicles. And yes, you could go into the street, but why would you want to?

The haven of the grass makes a lot more sense. Here is where you are safe; here is where you are *saved.* The street is scarcely of consequence, as it is not even a temptation; things are too good in the grass to wander into the street. The grass and the essence of the good things there are the motivation to stay away from the street. I know, it seems so simple, but I believe that it is God's intention for us as His beloved. No, not to try and stop sinning, but to not sin simply because we have it so good. The law made nothing perfect; we could try and stay out of the street, but our efforts didn't complete us. So a better way was introduced, and then we were no longer striving. We were whole and able to draw near to God (Hebrews 7:19). And now, the promise is fulfilled, the better way is that the law no longer exists in stone, it is written on our hearts, and that is what motivates us (Romans 2:15)!

And there I was, sitting on the green grass. It was good, but glimpses of my past and the current state of my butt, well, those things left me knowing what I was up against, and digging out would be a bigger battle than I would like to face. For a life free of condemnation, free from sin, I can see that He can rule in me and love on me; and yes, I want to stay in the green grass. Still, there is that voice, one that sings my failures and loathes my thighs. A voice that I knew understood a lot about me. How much I love rules, plans, and brand-new day planners with pens and highlighters and little "You did it!" stickers.

I could see there was a hope of coming to know how much I am truly adored by my Jesus. The question remained, would that equate to peace with my "flaws" or coming to a place where I recognized the completed work?

A girl would like to hope. . .so she did.

Well, Girl Wisdom

Shame has no place in your life. As a believer in Jesus Christ, we are welcomed to freedom. And yet, so many add-ons keep us in bondage to ourselves in the shame game. Are you holding on to past hurts or mistakes? Do you believe you are wholly loved as a daughter by a Father who created you in His image? Under the law, we were held hostage to our works. Under the New Covenant, we were set free. Everything we need is available to us right now, here in the green grass. What keeps you from wandering into the street? Are you tempted because you believe you can't? Or are you free because you don't want to be outside of God's good and perfect plan for you?

Freedom Gain

I have drunk deeply of shame for many years. Recently, I thought of something from my past. I almost immediately realized I was free of that mess. I didn't cry or criticize myself. As a matter of fact, I was grateful for the mistake. It hurt at the time, but I am better for it now. Take a few moments to think about shame. Write it out. Do you need to be set free? Ask for freedom. Do you need to see yourself through God's eyes? Ask Him. I believe He will set you free.

CHAPTER THREE

Stone-Cold Saved

*"You were tired out by the length of your road,
yet you did not say, 'It is hopeless.' You found
renewed strength, therefore you did not faint."*
ISAIAH 57:10 NASB

I have not had a good night's sleep since May of
1995. Next to pie and lipstick, sleep is my obsession. I believe my husband and I to be sleep mongrels.
We will do it anywhere, at any time, with anyone. We
just want to sleep. And yes, I signed up for overtime,
volunteer motherhood through foster care, but honestly, I did so while sleep-deprived.

I find sleep one of our Creator's most brilliant innovations. Sleep and the platypus are but a glimpse
at His mastermind. I imagine Him fashioning Adam
together and then sitting back and thinking, *"This is
good, but I think he should be unconscious for seven to
nine hours at a time. While in this state, I will let his
brain do crazy things as a form of rest. I am not really
going to make unicorns or leprechauns, but I will allow
dreams to manifest them, and then man can put visions
of them in books. Yes, this is good."*

To this end, I am always fascinated when people do not believe in God or an all-powerful Maker.

I mean, all the blood vessels, fingernails, eyelashes, just so many teeth, and where babies come from? To imagine that as happenstance is lost on me. I can't help but see the perfect design, the masterful intricacies, and the specific formula that is a glimpse at a divine love.

And to me, this is good.

This is the place where we get a vivid glimpse of our heavenly creative Father. As I prepared this chapter, I sat on the dock at my parents' lake house. It was a gorgeous day. Puffs of white scattered across the crisp spring sky. They decorated the day without an ounce of acknowledgment for uniformity, yet they breathed a tendency for monotony. The temperature was a perfect 78 degrees. As I sat, mesmerized by the soft laps of water against the mossy bulkhead, I prayed, "How can I convince them?"

How can I make you understand the depth of love God has for you? This perfect God, who thought of everything? When we finally get this love, when we understand this, it will change everything. It will take away shame; it will silence insecurities and get our feet out of the "come Monday" mentality. This love will override every barrier we have for staying in unhealthy places.

And it occurred to me, I can't offer you something I do not have. At that moment, it was most obvious: I haven't fully embraced the love He has for me. So I asked Him to show me. And I sat impatiently and waited.

A lanky, gray sandhill crane swooped down and plucked a small catfish out of the lake. I would call him Ichabod. Ichabod Crane did so with grace and ease and then came to a gliding and masterful landing on the moist and dewy lawn. He ignored me as he devoured his fresh-caught lunch. I was again struck by the perfection, the circle of life. To my right, my dad's purple martin condo was alive with chirps from newly hatched little ones. The new bird parents were busy in and out of the prebuilt nests. Suddenly, a fluffy squirrel dashed across the damp grass and then scampered up an enormous pine tree, another chased after her.

Such dynamic simplicity amidst such outstanding complexities.

Scripture states, "Are not two sparrows sold for a penny? Yet not one of them will fall to the ground outside your Father's care. And even the very hairs of your head are all numbered. So don't be afraid; you are worth more than many sparrows" (Matthew 10:29–31). And I am certain many who read this book will have heard that verse, some may have even memorized it, but do you believe it?

Friend, are you weary? The tedium, formality, and pomp and circumstance of religion cannot hold a candle to the magnificent dance of relationship. We can bow and kneel, we can fold our hands and do it all just so, but the law didn't ever set us free. Jesus did. There is a place, comfortable and familiar, where you know *of God*. You know the words to the songs, the accustomed cadence of the scripture, and the musty attar of the worn sanctuary carpet. But without throwing aside the normalcy and importance of this thing called the church, step into the light of *knowing God*. Oh yes, to know OF God is much different than KNOWING God.

For a moment, breathe in the reality of the Creator as His beloved created. Inhale and fill your lungs with the power of life. Life, as we prowl about, is often neglected in all its majesty. The ease by which we breathe is rarely considered unless we get an upper respiratory infection or must put laundry away on the second story. I know, I did this for years. I found myself doing all the things all the time and then I was mystified as to why God wasn't more careful with me.

If He loved me, why did bad things happen?

While I held these questions at bay out of terror or reverence, the words reverberated, "Jesus, I need help to be better." Have you wondered the same thing? Have you questioned where God was, why horrible things happened, and why He didn't answer?

I created a cycle of defeat that separated me from a good and loving Father. Please stop and consider this; it is a tragedy among the body of Christ. A cycle that squashes motivation. It is the belief that our good or bad works somehow morph God into a good or bad God. Hear me now. He is just good. He is not out to get you. He is not ignoring you. God is for you—He is for your marriage, your relationship, your career, and your babies. *He is for you.* He is for your wholeness, your restoration, and your peace. Jesus didn't offer us a problem-free life. Nor is He the author of hardship. He offers us the promise He would make beauty from ashes.

If there were any scenario where He wasn't utterly crazy about you, He would have spared His beloved Jesus the agony of death on a cross. He is the playwright of triumph. He is the conductor of a majestic symphony, where you are shown the delight of His favor. He knows the plans He has for you, and the plans that He dictates are lovely and dear.

We are not in trouble.

All is not lost. There is no harm, no foul. He sees us, and He is pleased with us. You and I are His babies, His darling daughters, and nothing can separate us from His love. Nope, nothing, not even *that*. It is easy to mistake Him, for under the heavy hand of the law and the earthly understanding of "do good get good, do bad get bad," we are often left with a broken heart. For if we are good, why is there bad? This is performance-based love that we often project onto God because it's everywhere else in the world... and this keeps us trapped in old cycles because we're sure we're not doing enough right.

I now submit wholly to the notion of grace as described by Paul in Romans 3:20–24:

Therefore no one will be declared righteous in God's sight by the works of the law; rather, through the law we become conscious of our sin. But now apart from the law the righteousness of God has been made known, to which the Law and the Prophets testify. This righteousness is given through faith in Jesus Christ to all who believe. There is no difference between Jew and Gentile, for all have sinned and fall short of the glory of God, and all are justified freely by his grace through the redemption that came by Christ Jesus.

For God so loved us, He gave His only Son. The selfless act tore the temple veil, and it was no longer necessary for the priest to stand watch in the temple. The Lord Jesus Christ, the High Priest Himself, sat down. *He sat down.* And He is seated at the right hand of the Father (Hebrews 10:10–14). These are the basic truths of our Christian walk.

And this is where I want us to look into the face of Jesus, who would be nailed to a cross for our folly. This is the essence of His compassion, the girth of His love for us. This is the how and why. This is where we can find the courage to make changes in our lives for good.

Imagine yourself curled up on the hard, dry ground. Tears stain your face. Your heart is slamming in your chest and echoing in your ears. All around you are your accusers, and yes, some of them share your face, for you are your harshest critic. They hold heavy, smooth stones. Many of the stones are tinted with the blood of the victim from the last stoning.

This spot. . .this is where your prosecutors will deliver blow after blow to your body with the weighty rocks they clutch. This spot is one of terror. Your folly, the thing you hate most about yourself, is the thing that will magnify the bashes.

And He steps into the circle of your doom.

You dare not look up. You see His sandaled feet and the cuff of His well-worn robe. It is dusty and tattered from the miles you safely assume He has walked to come to this place, the place of your demise. The clarity of His question, the authority with which He speaks, is chilling. *"Whoever among you is without sin, you cast the first stone."* Without moving your downcast face, you peek to your right and left, and your accusers are dropping their stones. You see the stones fall, you see the dust erupt about them, and you hear your dejected assassins mumbling under their breath.

They will not be pummeling you; you have been spared.

Still paralyzed by a shaky reality, you shiver at the feet of your Savior. He holds His hand out for you to stand. You are visibly traumatized and place your trembling hand in His. It is warm, calloused, and you are moved to your core by the touch. He draws you to your feet. He is tall. You are looking up at this unbelievably gentle hero. His brown eyes hold a purity you have not known, and you question your ability to understand Him or the grace He now offers you. Still, *you do know Him.* Salty tears burn your eyes. One escapes and runs down your cheek, tracing its way through the dust on your face. You are desperate to look away for He is so good and you. . . *you are the worst.* Undeniably, you are suspended in a stare that you cannot break.

He speaks. *"Who is here to accuse you?"*

For the first time, you are cognizant of what is asked of you. Your eyes dart about the square, the place where you so nearly met with death.

All of your accusers are gone.

Your parched lips part and your voice is brittle from the near miss. From your throat, you muster the sounds, "No one?"

He smiles. Light and joy pour from Him, flooding you with the peace you do not recognize, yet welcome and pray is your new normal. Again, He speaks, *"Neither do I."* His rugged hand brushes the tear from your cheek. He places both hands on your shoulders to steady you. He is everything. He is the One. He is your Savior, and you are without words for the freedom He just delivered you.

Can you imagine? Can you pretend to see? Can you picture it? Can you breathe in the reality of He who stepped in and spoke on your behalf and saved you from this diabolical fate? *Friend, that is exactly what happened!* And even if it had just been you, He would have volunteered to lie down on that hard, tragic cross and die *just for you.* He is the hero we have been waiting for. He is the one who speaks on our behalf and exaggerates our beauty, talent, and abilities as grandly as a daddy in love with his blameless little girl. He would step into the stoning circle again and again that you might know this truth. What keeps you from believing you are blameless?

Whether you said yes to Him decades ago or just now, He set you apart for this salvation. He died for you. He loves you. And He does not accuse you! The world will always accuse us; God never will. The Good News is that the blood worked. There is nothing that can separate you from that love. The only thing that keeps us held hostage from this pure freedom is the mindset that we are about to be stoned to death! We believe we are the worst of the worst, unforgivable. And we cling to the belief that our sin is so much bigger than any other sin. Yet how could our sin be the last straw of a God whose wrath was already settled with the perfect sacrifice—His Son, Jesus.

This is the good stuff. Before our *yes* to Jesus, we were lost. Now we are found! And still, we wander about the universe trying to "get better." We strive and struggle to overcome that which was overcome on the cross! The stones are dropped. You have stood up and looked into the face of your Redeemer!

Your hero, brave warrior, prince, and gallant knight. . .He showed up. He did the hardest thing ever for you. You, His beloved.

This is where we can rest now, nestled down in the green grass. This was the promise. Peace, joy, and life abundant (John 10:10). I propose we said yes to

Jesus and then added a *but*. "Yes, Jesus, and I appreciate Your sacrifice, but I need to get my act together." And again in that instance, we add a *but* to the completed work of the cross.

"Yes, Jesus, I see You. I just need to get a few things nailed down, and then I will get back to You. Just let me fix these things that are wrong with me. Then, as soon as I can deserve Your lavish love, I will pencil You into my schedule and try and focus on the things You say about me. I have You arranged for "come Monday."

Let us go back to the town square where you have just been spared a brutal death. You have been saved. Saved, not "kind of" saved. No one is left to accuse you. However, instead of embracing this gift, you argue with the Savior. *"Who is here to accuse you?"* and you look about and say, "No one, but You have no idea what a mess I am!" We have invited the would-be assassins back into the stoning circle, begging them to stand with the threat should you fall out of line!

We are baffled and exhausted from the struggle, from the fear of accusation, accusation that we were spared! Round and round Christian women spin about in the town square, waiting to be stoned to death when they have already been bought and paid for! Oh, friend, this is the place we have been invited to rest! This is the place where there is no condemnation. There are no accusers.

You are free.

This is the place you belong. You have found the

safety you crave. You just need to look about and see there is no one here to accuse you. You are welcome here. You are saved.

Rest now.

OLD HABITS

Some habits are harder to break than others, but we serve a God of the impossible. He walks on water, turns water into wine, and rises from the dead. He wants us to believe in the boundlessness of His mercy.

When we are primed and ready for trouble and believe that is what we are in, we are so much more susceptible to the lie "You need to get it together." Recently I was staying at my parents' home on the lake. Our two sons, Sam and Charlie, "the Vandals," were sleeping in the guest room next to mine. I was awakened with a jolt as a loud alarm was set off. I jumped out of bed, rushed to the hallway, and met the two startled little boys. They had wide eyes, and their hands shielded their little ears from the blaring noises.

They yelled over the ear-splitting panic, "WE DIDN'T DO IT! WE WAS ASLEEP IN DA BEDS! MOMMY, WE DIDN'T DO IT! WE PWOMISE!"

Bless. How many alarms have the Vandals set off? How many fires? Broken eggs, jars of peanut butter destroyed, toilets clogged, vacuums disman-tled, shattered windows, cats shaved, and carpets re-placed. . .and yet, they were blameless.

Here is the place we must recognize we are blameless.

I know it isn't easy. I know we have been told, through seemingly ordained messages, of our wretchedness. And believe me, I understand the fine line between the humble Christianese of unworthiness and the battle cry of the redeemed and adored. It is a hard place; we don't want to sound ungrateful or pompous, but at the same time. . .who are we to deny what Christ has done for us and who He says we are?

To accuse the church of confusing the issue seems as though we are treading on the irreverent. But it is for such a time as this, we absolutely must start speaking up for who we are, believing the wholeness of the Gospel and stopping the nonsense that the church has perpetuated for ages about women, our place, our rights, and who we are. I fully believe it is this place of confusion that has separated us from our identity, left us hiding in our closets eating our feelings, and even worse, left us to be victimized, molested, violated, and silenced in the very place we should have been most loudly heard and entirely safe. Choosing to move forward into a healthy mindset and body requires us to participate. It means we must make some decisions. It means we know WHO we are because of Jesus and cling to this with all we have until it becomes our new normal.

Before we go any further, I am moved to have that be our prayer:

Heavenly Father, how we need You. Let every lovely eye that falls upon this feel the immense freedom bought when You stepped into the square and stopped the stoning. Look at us. Search our hearts, our minds, and the desperate need we have for You and FILL US UP! That is the promise, and You know us. You created us to give. We have given so much to those around us, to our children, spouses, the church, our neighbors. Here we are now, a sisterhood depleted. Prepare us for this new journey, fill us up, overflowing, pressed down, shaken together as we have given, please give it back now. Open our eyes to this newfound truth, help our unbelief, and protect as we move forward into the liberty You alone can deliver. The enemy would love to leave us here, tormenting us with the stoning. . .we claim victory and bind him to the foot of the cross. In Jesus' name, amen.

These first three chapters have outlined many of the reasons we stay stuck in unhealthy patterns. Just so we're on the same page, let's review them here for quick reference. You may need to review this list from time to time to make sure these aren't in play in your life. Because when they are, healthy living is hard because we struggle to believe we deserve it. I am here to testify, you deserve wellness. He died so that you might live. Now that we've identified unhealthy patterns, let's look at why we must leave them behind. Here's what's available to you. . .*woman.*

Well, Girl Wellness

So let's review.

1. We aren't starting over. We are in a relationship with a God who died for us. He loves us. He knows us. We are moving forward.
2. Shame is out the window. How can we be ashamed of the creation where Jesus dwells? Shame tactics are from the devil. We will keep recognizing them for what they are and rejecting them.
3. Beloved Living is our goal.
    a. Seek Him in all things.
    b. Discern what we think, what we believe about ourselves, God, and the factors that influence those beliefs.
    c. Make genuine peace with yourself by accepting the truth of who you are in Jesus.

Freedom Gain

Stop and think about freedom and salvation. The entirety of why Jesus died was so that we might be free. Take a minute to write out the truth of your salvation. Ask God to open your eyes to the whole truth of who He is and what that means about what He did for you out of pure love. No buts.

For a free printable download of Beloved Living principles visit www.sacredgroundstickyfloors.com/wellgirlresources.

CHAPTER FOUR

Woman

God is within her, she will not fall.
PSALM 46:5

*O*ur youngest Vandal son, Charlie, calls me "woman." He doesn't do it all the time, but every time he does, it cracks me up. Recently he was trying to explain something to me, and he barked, "WOMAN! Youms not wistening to me!" I posted the conversation on social media, and there was only one negative comment. "I cannot believe you would let your child talk like that to you." Yeah, well, I am a woman. Charlie calls it like he sees it.

No one else in my life calls me this; I don't know where he got it. But it inspired this chapter title, and I feel like this is one of the most important chapters in this book. It's pivotal. We've just dug in and unearthed the things that have kept us stuck for so long. I'm proud of you for digging with me. It takes guts to look at those roots—ones that have been there for so long and are so deep. But now we're switching gears and taking the next step toward new living. This chapter holds some baggage. As women, we are handed quite a bit of baggage in the ways of protecting ourselves, respecting ourselves, respecting the men in our lives, and teaching our daughters, nieces, and other young girls we encounter the validity of their design.

And this is a wellness book. But how many of us have tried all the wellness tricks, and here we are, reading another wellness book? I propose this is because we never get to the root, or the bottom of the well, and unpack all the aspects of wellness. I can't help but think of the woman at the well. Jesus said to her, "Woman. . ." He knew her. He knew everything about her, and He called her *woman*. He offered her freedom and salvation. For the first time, she had the answer. We have the answer too. His name is Jesus, and He calls us "woman."

If I am to be completely candid with you, the three women who first read this chapter quickly recognized that my wounds, as a woman, were voiced in toxicity. Not that we shouldn't have a voice, but mine cracked with the pangs of my past. As I read through it and these trusted friends' observations, I saw it too. Which brings me to the objective of this chapter: love. Scripture tells us that we should love our neighbor as we love ourselves (Matthew 22:39). Most of the time when this scripture is shared, the focus is on loving our neighbor. But I want to start at the end of the verse and ask you this question: Do you love who you are? And were you to write a book, would your words be healthy? Or laced with contempt? Ah, yes, I told you, I was unraveling with you.

Let me start here. I am all about strong, moral,

decent men. I believe that God's design, man and woman, is perfect. Because face it, He is perfect. He knew what He was doing when He created the sexes. At the same time, I am all about strong, moral, decent women. I want us to stay focused. Our focus for this book is Jesus, wellness, and freedom. And I believe Jesus is the answer to all the wellness and freedom we need.

Furthermore, I find nothing humorous in man-bashing. To me, it is as offensive as pornography. The old adage "Boys will be boys" is objectionable to me. And yet, I subscribed to a nature in my wounded wording that condoned a stereotypical dialogue. "Women will be bitter, rebellious, and snarky?" Nah. In a perfect world, boys will be men who respect women and are of good moral character, with a heart that seeks to know the God of his creation. And girls will be women of compassion, tenderness, mercy, wisdom, and chase the God of their creation with grit and grace.

Amen.

As I went back through this chapter, I saw something I am sure my friends most readily recognized. Having had an opportunity to sit with Jesus, process what my friends were saying, and check it against the Word, this is what I saw: *rebellion*. I submit that rebellion is born of oppression, discrimination, and abuse. Somewhere along the way, some incident, harsh word, or hurt did a work in me, where the woman I am was transformed, albeit temporarily, into a venomous rebel.

I have a strong voice. I have opinions, obviously. But this chapter had more relevance than I could have known. Because there is a difference between advocacy and rebellion.

So where is the balance I crave? Isn't wellness balance? Well, let me start by saying what I am seeing is that passion is part of my design. I have always been passionate about women bettering themselves. And I have always wanted to contribute to the cause. I propose the majority of us are motivated by our trials. *What I don't want for you or me is for us to be so marred by our past that our future is not a testament to the wholeness Jesus bought and paid for us.* And we can easily be divided on what feminist means or meant. All I have to say about that is this: there is no sage conclusion where I should burn my bra. Also, I am pro armpit shaving. You cannot talk me out of that.

God knows His children. He knows how to reach them. He knows what they need and who they need it from. He knows you. He knows your passion, and He knows what brought you to that conclusion. And I trust Him. I trust Him to go with us on this wellness journey, show us what we are missing and why, and heal us completely. I am undone by woman. She was created as companion. My companions were able to see what I could not, something that might have cost many readers the advantages of this freedom because my hurt and insurgence seeped onto the page. How do we not let our pain seep out and onto the pages of our life?

Remember, I'm writing this as I walk the same path as you do, asking God to heal my broken heart as He makes me whole. The friends who helped shape this chapter remind me that we really are in this together. And I hope you realize that you and I are too.

How Do You View Womanhood?

I have never doubted that being a woman wasn't the best choice God could make for a girl such as myself. What I want us to consider is how we view our womanhood. Think about it: Are you glad to be a woman? Have you ever felt shame or fear because you are a woman? Have you ever been discriminated against as a woman?

At one point in my college education, I had started a doctoral program. When I told my grandfather about the possibility of earning a PhD, he asked me, "How does someone address an envelope to a man and wife if the wife is a doctor?" And I said, "I guess, Mr. and Dr.?" No kidding, he said, "But then won't people think the Mr. is a homosexual?" Oh. My. Stars. God love my grandpa, he grew up in a day when women just weren't doctors. I giggle at the story now, but I told that story once in mixed company and was met with boos and hisses.

In an "us versus them" society, rebellion is bred. And this is hard. If a person feels threatened, they will either flee or rise up. I now realize neither of these has to be exclusive to our womanhood. We can champion each other, we can have strong opinions, and we matter. What I don't want to negate is our per-fected design for the fury. Granted, some of us have earned the right to rise up and rage. Which brings me to the fury part. What I think happened in the first draft of this chapter was that I raged and ranted so I didn't have to submit to the hurt of healing. My guess is you've done the same things somewhere in your life too. So let's dig a little deeper. Together I want to walk through some of my hurts and chew on some of yours and see where we end up.

I recently had coffee with an acquaintance, and her college-aged daughter stopped in the coffee shop to pick up some papers from her mother, my coffee date. The young woman was pleasant and hur-ried. After she left, I asked her mom about the girl's T-shirt. The shirt had a derogatory reference to male genitalia scrolled across it. I found it most odd be-cause this girl has an amazing father and three fan-tastic older brothers, all who adore her. And I think that is exactly how I inquired, "Why would someone like 'Beth' have such a harsh shirt? Her daddy and brothers are so amazing?!"

My coffee date looked down at her coffee, her eyes filled with tears, and she said, "She was raped. Her first week at another college. That's why she moved home. We don't tell anyone." I think I was only able to whimper, "Me too." To which my friend re-sponded, "Yeah. . .me too."

As I worked on this and how to appropriately convey my message, I read a Tweet from author, pastor, and counselor Bob Hamp: "At the foundation of all abuse is the inappropriate assignment of responsibility." Yeah. . .me too. When I was fourteen, I was assaulted at a public swimming pool by an eighteen-year-old boy. Later, someone who knew him said, "Well, he thought you were sixteen because you are so developed." For years I questioned this. *If only I had. . .* But the truth was, he had no right to touch me against my will no matter my age. There is no excuse *ever* for a violation against you. And we must shout this from the rooftops, for it is paramount in making peace with our bodies. Our bodies are not too much, not enough, or anything—no nothing but the grand design of a good and loving Father. And He intended that we are protected, loved, and whole. Friend, it's imperative we grab hold of this truth for it's foundational to becoming wholehearted and healthy.

In graduate school, I had to take a class on cultural femininity. Of course this would involve enormous extremes, like the burka, the heavy black drape that many eastern-culture women wear, even in 120-degree weather. Foremost in my mind is a documentary we watched about a desolate village in Asia.

There were no girls. So shamed by the birth of a daughter, the fathers would drown the baby girls upon delivery. They wanted only sons. And now, after years of this barbaric practice, there were no wives to produce sons for all the sons. It seems like common sense, right? But no, this had evaded this little village that would soon meet with extinction for the lack of women. We matter. And, no, not just to give birth. But we are part of a perfect design, created for life. Yes, I see you, a woman who has not been able to conceive. Dear one, I am so sorry. You are heard and seen. I do not know why this has not happened for you, but it does not negate your life or your value. It most certainly does not count you as less in the eyes of the Father. I have stopped to cry now and pray that you are answered.

And you who do not want children, okay? So your Creator did not put that desire in your heart. There is no shame in this. The world will be quick to question you, "Sooo??? When are you going to have a baby?" Really, this is so offensive. I think a proper response is, "You mean when am I going to have productive sex? Is that what you are asking me? 'Cause right now, we are just mating for fun. But I can email you if things change."

Your identity is in Christ alone. Not the contents or lack of your uterus.

Women are part of the grand and perfect design that our Father in heaven *planned*. The world and its wayward interpretations and of who we are and all the abuses may have knocked the wind out of your sails, but Jesus came to breathe life back into them.

This is the fight song I pray is manifested by this script: *you matter. These two words have the power to unlock the prison of lies and insecurities we've lived in for so long.* No matter what anyone has said or done to you, you matter. Jesus is all in for your restoration. He loves you. He chose you as woman; He knows you. Sit with Him, without expectation or highlighter or pen. Just sit. Focus on His face in the town square, when He interceded on your behalf and reminded you there were no accusers around, holding stones designed to hurt you. Fall into the arms of the Jesus who loves you, His girl, above all. I know it is hard to drown out the voices and the lies, but if you let His voice be the only one you hear, He will win out in the end. He promises if you ask, and seek, you will find (Matthew 7).

This balance champions for the cause of our womanhood and looks different than rebellious activism. No, we cannot grow weary for the work is so important; we have been invited to a time where finally speaking out "ME TOO and NEVER YOU" are some of the most important words we can muster. Simultaneously, what I now see is that His intent is never bitterness. This is what my friends caught as they read this chapter. And I'm so glad they did because there is a balance He has for us. A balance that is achieved in wholly seeking Him, letting Him heal us, guide us, and make us whole. For me, in a book about wellness, balance is absolutely paramount. He alone is the way, the truth, and the life.

The S Word

Submission. The mere mention of the word might have sent you reeling. It sat wrong with me, apparently. But I want to take a fresh look at submission and how it pertains to Beloved Living. Remember, Beloved Living is seeking God in everything. And remembering though everything is permissible, is it beneficial? It is embracing that which is our inheritance, true freedom, and salvation. It is feasting with Him, believing Him. And when we love, we are willing to submit to that love. When we choose to love God, then we have the motivation to submit to His will and ways. We trust that love. It casts out all fear. It is patient, it is kind. . .

> It does not envy, it does not boast, it is not
> proud. It does not dishonor others, it is not
> self-seeking, it is not easily angered, it keeps no
> record of wrongs. Love does not delight in evil
> but rejoices with the truth. It always protects,
> always trusts, always hopes, always perseveres.
> Love never fails. But where there are prophe-
> cies, they will cease; where there are tongues,
> they will be stilled; where there is knowledge,
> it will pass away. (1 Corinthians 13:4–8)

And submitting to this, I am on board.

Where I was wrong in the first draft was my rebellion against submission. And this is where I needed to be called out in love and be healed of my hurts. Because the examples I am going to share with you are not submission out of love. I recall a very hard season after our youngest daughter, Sophie, was born. She was two weeks old when I was readmitted to the hospital for an emergency hysterectomy. Shortly after my hysterectomy and extended recovery, I attended a support group for women with endometriosis and chronic pelvic pain. It was held in a church basement, and of the eleven women in the group, four of them were "submitting" to painful intercourse because their pastor told them they had to. Jesus, help. This is no highway to a healthy marriage. The meetings were laced with heartbreaking accounts of resentment toward their partner, physical agony, and a definite belief they were not cared for, nor did their well-being matter to a God who demanded they meet the needs of their husband at all costs.

I am undone by the tragedy of this teaching, but I also fully believe we are moving away from it. But in the presence of a "have to" mindset, marriages are continually robbed of mutual pleasure and connection that accompanies a respectful partnership and healthy sexual relationship. One where reverence and desire are nonnegotiable in a mutual chorus of companionship. Additionally, I believe the majority of good husbands would prefer not to force their wives into an encounter they were not interested in, or worse, caused them physical and/or emotional pain. And worse than that lousy submission story, I had a childhood friend who was molested by her pastor. When she told her mother, her mom confronted her with the Old Testament scripture about submission. Holy Moses.

That is not submission.

So, the scripture in Ephesians 5, where Paul speaks about submission, is the Greek term for "voluntarily putting oneself under the authority of the head of household,"[1] as Christ does. Note that it was not a military ranking term. And it was followed by "Husbands love your wives as Christ does the church" and "submitted or gave Himself up to her."

Gave Himself up to her.

Abuse followed by biblical privilege is not from Jesus. Abuse, followed by any justification, is not license to abuse. It is the perpetrator's burden, and he or she will have to face the God of justice. I wish there were pages I could dedicate to building you up, showing you the wholeness bought for you on Calvary, but I trust Jesus to use these words to start a fire. We matter.

You matter.

Woman was created for commitment and loyalty. She was fashioned to follow while leading with passion, adoration, and love. Which brings me to Ruth. While she had not borne any children and her husband was now gone, Ruth would not leave her mother-in-law. I have heard this Bible story from the book of Ruth since childhood. The woman who was the epitome of loyalty, who would follow Naomi, mother of Ruth's deceased husband, to her homeland. Before this prose, I guess I believed this was a story about getting good out of the bad, that obedience

---

[1] https://en.wikipedia.org/wiki/Oikos accessed on 8/7/2019.

would lead to reward.

I have since changed my mind.

Ruth shows us the fruit of submission.

This was Ruth's act of submission. When her husband and father-in-law and brother-in-law passed, Ruth gave up her family, her country, her laws, and her future and submitted out of love, not law. Anything we do in love is going to be a more pleasing offering. I submit to Justin because I love Justin. Just as Justin submits to me because he loves me. And I come to you with humility and love; I have a happy marriage. Notice, I did not say a perfect one. Justin and I have had good seasons and seasons that were reminiscent of an armpit in both smell and the sticky, sweaty, hairy, and altogether grossness.

But the point is not even marriage, it is submitting to God because we love Him. It is trusting Him to guide us in what is for us and what is not radical trust. It's trusting His motives and heart. Ruth's submission was an act of love and mercy.

While Eve would be accused all the ages of being the downfall, she was, in fact, the key to the story of who we are as women. God called her "Mother of all the Living." And even if you love on a cat or fern, you were created to nurture. Ruth has been the biblical model of women for years, giving herself up for love. This is who we are. We are self-sacrificing beings. But again, I call you to look at balance; without it, we are not truly well.

If we only give of ourselves, we will run dry. If we

only serve ourselves, we are not living as Christ lived. Philippians 2:7 (NLT) reads, "Instead, [Jesus] gave up his divine privileges; he took the humble position of a slave and was born as a human being." He then died and was exalted to the highest place of honor, seated at the right hand of the Father. There is a time for us to serve, and there is a time for us to rest. We needn't rebel to advocate. We don't have to burn a bra or picket to protest. And in all things, we are called to love. Again, perfect love casts out all fear. At the root of much rebellion is fear. Let us not be afraid of the healing love of Jesus.

The love of Jesus is everything. That is what He left us: love one another. And I believe that He created us companions. Humanity seems to be the interfering factor. I am convinced the teaching that women are secondary is dangerous. Its damage is so far-reaching that I fully believe this is the work of the enemy to distort the truth and spread the lie that women do not matter. I also believe this seeps into our lives and makes us question our value in God's plan, right?

Very important women in my life were essential in me rewriting this chapter. In the process, I saw my open wounds. And this is my hope for you too, that your eyes will be open to all that God has in store for you when you submit to His healing and leading. There is safety in submitting to Him. I am in no way downplaying or neglecting your hurts. But heaven knows, I downplayed and neglected mine. They manifested in a rant that allowed me to sound wise and ignore the healing I needed. This is my hope for you that you can find balance in your womanhood. That you can be all the things, because really, that is what a woman is. She is strong and weak, loud and quiet, grace and grit; she is a montage of oxymorons. And this can be a real blessing when balance is applied. We needn't be victimized in our femininity, and we needn't negate our femininity to voice our concerns.

Womanhood in Action

So in this unraveling, where does food, wellness, and body image come into play? Well, I believe it comes in action, in what is for us and what is not for us. So in the first draft of this chapter, I was a woman. . . you could have heard me roar and snarl and foam at the mouth. In the second draft, I was forced to look deeper at why this was my reaction to my womanhood. Obviously, I have exposed some of my baggage. And just like my friend's daughter with the obscene T-shirt, I have a great dad. I have an amazing husband. I have raised good and decent sons who respect and honor women. I am in the process of doing that again. And I have met with abuse, discrimination, and I have been both afraid and ashamed of my womanhood.

I slammed my laptop shut at least thirteen times in this composition. I went looking for a snack. Then I went looking for a cigarette, and I don't smoke. I cried. I watched YouTube animated videos of my favorite podcast, and then I rummaged through the pantry again. And then I remembered something: I can't stuff one feeling and feel another. I was hurting. I was hurting for the injustices, mine and yours. I was afraid my words wouldn't be enough to convince me or you how much we are loved, how worthy we have been counted, and how fully we can be set free. And I had a choice: I could rebel or I could submit.

I could try and do things my way, be like Eve. . .go back to the Tree of Good and Evil for one more bite and "get better." I could stay crippled with insecurity or snarling with pride and risk health and wholeness, or I could submit to the God who knows I am woman and still calls me His.

In an eerie turn of events, I went into my room and climbed onto the bed and stared at the ceiling and waited for the assault of things I knew I should probably feel. And I got a text from one of the three women who had counseled me on this very chapter. It was a picture of her youngest daughter, at a bookstore, holding one of my books. The little girl is about the same age as the little girl who called me mommy for two years before she was removed from our home and returned to her restored mama.

Before I could even respond, my dad texted me from an event. He was telling me that someone at his table read my book and was raving about it. I sent him the picture I had just received, a little muppet holding my book. And my dad responded, "Oh, baby, I am sorry."

If my earthly daddy could sense that I was coming undone, can you imagine what my heavenly Father sees and knows? And that is what I was left with: I needed to come undone in the arms of my Father.

So I did.

I grieved like a boss. No, please don't call it crying like a girl. I hate that branding. I fell apart, not because I am weak; I fell apart because I needed the reprieve of grief, because I am strong 99 percent of the time. I was created sensitive. I was not created "victim." I was created woman, and I came to serve not to be served. But yes, open my door, take out the trash, and go ahead, pay for my dinner. I want to be heard, but I also want to listen.

I will rally the troops, but we will also hold a quiet vigil.

Woman, you are all the things. All those things matter and are good. And in the scope of balance, that means feeling all the feels. I propose we use food, drink, and plans to control that which is complete insanity. And while it was painful to expose some of what I have had to expose here, I am better for it. After that last sentence, I went outside and threw rocks in the lake for thirty minutes. I felt this pent-up energy and frustration leaving my body, and I recognized I used to stuff that. If you have stuffed things too, you know what I am talking about. My limbs tingled as I threw rock after rock. And I was further stunned by this.

What are we missing? What energies are festering in us? And by energies, I mean the tangible feelings we have when we are faced with our past or injustices. Are you stuffing those feelings? Or experiencing them? Are you rebelling? Or are you a peaceable advocate? Are you willing to listen to wise counsel? Are you capable of submitting to wisdom when it stares you in the face? What motivates you? And why?

Obviously, I believe God. I believe He can make all things new, no matter how worn out you feel. I have witnessed this, and maybe you have too. And while these words have been harder than any I have ever written, they keep coming. At 3:00 a.m. I woke in a sweat, there are so many parts to this. And I felt all the pangs of birthing something new. I sat bolt upright in bed and said out loud, "Jesus, please help me."

I woke the next morning refreshed, full of hope and enthusiasm for this book that had me giddy with the title for the next chapter. . ."How to Make Apple Pie."

Read on, baby girl.

Well, Girl Wisdom

How do you feel about your womanhood? Are you stuffing? Are you raging? Do you recognize the difference?

Freedom Gain

Take a few moments to grieve. From this page forward, when we are wounded, let us fall into the arms of the God who came to save us.

CHAPTER FIVE

How to Make Apple Pie

So don't be misled, my dear brothers and sisters.
Whatever is good and perfect is a gift coming down to
us from God our Father, who created all the lights in the
heavens. He never changes or casts a shifting shadow.
He chose to give birth to us by giving us his true word.
And we, out of all creation, became his prized possession.
JAMES 1:16–18 NLT

So, what is it that makes you, you? What makes me, me?

I can't say I have always been bold. I cannot tell you that I was drenched in confidence. However, I can say, I believe in a Jesus who died for you and me, just as we are. And yes, I know that doesn't make my butt look any better, but I feel like it is essential in the quest for peace with bodies that won't cooperate with what we consider "perfect."

I recently received a letter from a disgusted reader. She accused me of showboating my adopted sons for the praise of man. Her words were harsh, and she believed that I was doing a huge disservice to my sons by referring to them as "adopted." She inquired, "Why can't they just be your children? Why must you call them out as secondary?" I was deeply troubled by this. It is never my intent to offend. (What? It's not.) That night I lay awake stewing over the lashing. Then, suddenly, I had a response.

They are adopted.

They are my sons. . .but I did not give birth to them. I have been given an opportunity, one I did not seek out on my own, to write about adoption and foster care. If I never gave my audience an opportunity to know the origin of Sam and Charlie's placement into our lives, my readers wouldn't come to me asking for advice, prayer, help, and encouragement. In our efforts to be sensitive and politically correct, we often miss the bigger picture of who we are. I am a mother of biological and adopted children. I am the daughter of Don and Glenna and the adopted daughter of Yahweh, who calls me His "prized possession" (James 1:18 NLT).

Who are you?

And then, just as I came to peace with my response, my phone lit up with a Facebook message. It read, "Jami, I am at the hospital with my first foster placement, a nineteen-hour-old baby boy. He is drug-addicted; he was abandoned here. The doctor just came in and said that he will not live through the night. His heart is failing. I am both shattered and honored to be here. . .but I feel I might die as I watch the monitor growing faint. How can I be this destroyed over a boy I just met? Please, pray for him and me. . . . He has no name, but you and I will call him Daniel."

Daniel.

Had I never made our foster care and adoption story public, I would have missed this opportunity to pray with and love Daniel and his "foster" mommy. A woman I now call friend and a child we grieve together. His story, the things that made Daniel, the evil that destroyed him, and the Father who welcomed him home are part of who I am. Our story, the ingredients, the finite details that developed us into whoever we are, they are important facts, anecdotes of why we react or fail to because of this or that. And no, every time I interact with Sam and Charlie, I don't point out their adoption, but it is a part of who they are. Their story is a part of my story, and it is a story I love to share.

Yes, there are things we wish to forget, scars that we beg to leave us. But I propose that those are still ingredients in the essence of you, and they matter. That awful stuff is stuff you survived. Which makes you a survivor. You are a perfect design, wandering about in a less-than-perfect world. Coming face-to-face with those ingredients, acknowledging them, is critical in the efforts of peace. I confess as I began this composition, I attended a meeting related to the topic of food addiction. After several sessions, I met with a seasoned participant to go over what I was learning and feeling.

Honestly, I felt like I was in a good place. I thought, "This is progress." But I was met with hostility and shame tactics. Praise God, I saw it for exactly what it was. A manipulative exercise in controlling behaviors by shaming the person. As I investigated further, I came to the realization that shame was the prime ingredient in the methodology. Berating myself and allowing others to try and expose me as guilty were supposedly the tactic by which I would be made whole.

A few years ago, I would have given them all of me, a blood oath if you will. However, since I have met with the Real Jesus and have come to understand He loves me, there is no condemnation. I bolted from the meeting and never looked back.

And that is who I am.

The DNA, the skin, and ligaments that hold me together are on purpose, an intentional design. And that is most certainly true of you as well. We are created with resolve, for worship, and for intimacy with a God who adores us. And here in this ingredient list, there may be some things that need to be acknowledged and others we can just look blatantly at and say, "I am done with that, it was overcome on the cross. . .I am moving on."

Heed the warning, to constantly dwell on our sin and the mistakes of our past is to neglect the freedom bought for us on the cross. By no means am I saying that the violation or pain you've endured is not a part of you; but I am saying God sees you as whole and will empower you to do the same. It is easy to fall prey to the idea you need to be "fixed." Most of our energies are spent trying to be better, different. The

Good News I am uncovering is that I am different. I was made different when I said "Yes!" to Jesus and fell into His arms and welcomed the gift of salvation. Different is good.

When we add up all the things that make us who we are, the list is going to be diverse. No one is going to be exactly the same, and the truth is, that is *amazing*. Do you know how many people are wandering on this big rock? And there is no one like you. There is no one with your story, *no one*. There is a precision that is accomplished in a recipe. If you vary it one way or the other, it is no longer the same thing. To that end, you can't force an apple pie recipe to become braised pork tenderloin. Furthermore, you can't make yourself whole and complete without Jesus. Jesus is the ingredient that makes you different, set apart, and infallible.

When we go to work on ourselves and use man-made tactics to "be better," we are trying to make pork tenderloin with apple pie ingredients. Of all the things I have learned about myself from the standpoint of perfection through Christ, this is paramount. An apple tree doesn't try and make apples, it just does. We sign up for these studies, trying to be more, better, and produce ALL the fruits of the spirit and yet continually fail. Why? Well, because we are not capable of producing apples.

The fruits of the spirit come from the Spirit. When the entirety of our focus is on the Spirit of God, those characteristics are our nature. The regular rules do not apply to those of us in the Spirit. We are entirely different; there is a change, like sugar dissolving in water, and it cannot be undone. It can be poked and prodded at, and it can sink to the bottom and make a syrupy mess, but a "yes" to Jesus is the ingredient that changes us into a new concoction.

Undone

Years ago as a kindergarten teacher, I had a little girl in my class with a severe birth defect. Her stomach was actually on the outside of her body. She had a feeding tube, and because of several surgeries and resulting scar tissue, no belly button. Our class went on a field trip to a Creation-based museum where the speaker told the children about their grand design and how God perfected them as His beloved. All was happy, goosebumpy, and glowy, until the speaker said, "Raise your hand if you have a belly button." In the crowd, there was no way to see "Susie" didn't raise her hand. Then the jazzy, sharply dressed speaker expounded, "Well then! If you have a belly button, YOU are a child of God! And if you don't, I guess you belong to the devil or are an alien."

Insert slow-motion special effects of me trying to tackle this woman and wrestle the microphone away from her. Alas, it was too late, the damage was done. Susie sat quietly and wept, wholly believing the lie she belonged to the devil or was an alien. There the little muppet sat, pigtails with impossibly huge coordinating bows balanced on her little strawberry-blond head, in a perfectly matching sundress with identical bloomers and ruffled socks. Susie's mom and dad did all they could to make her feel as special as they believed her to be. A life saved, cherished, a life that was at the core of everything that made their family, a family.

The teacher next to me whispered, "Well, that was lovely, she will *NEVER* get over that." And there is the biggest lie that we buy into. That we cannot recover, that we cannot be restored. Friend, have you bought the lie you cannot recover?

I pushed through the crowd and grabbed Susie and texted her mom. We spent all of our energies and every trick in the book to undo the damage to her tiny broken heart. The speaker was horrified at the realization and did her best to try and fix it. Also, I can promise she won't use that routine ever again.

Still, it is an ingredient in the story of Susie.

I believe that our efforts to assure her of how much she was loved and how she was created by a God who adores her did not go to waste. However, there is only one answer to life's wounds and the enemy's lies. His name is Jesus.

Our oldest daughter, Maggie, was recently diagnosed with celiac disease. She is not simply gluten-intolerant; she becomes gravely ill from even the smallest dose of wheat. And we, her family and friends, are happy to make accommodations for her. I use this example as a segue to being accommodating to the people you encounter who don't know

Christ. While Jesus is my entirety, He is not everyone's. Some people have deep wounds that are aggravated by the mere mention of His name. What I want to clarify here is that He is cool with that. Remain calm. He knows His children. He wants restoration and wholeness for His creation. So while you and I might be able to lean fully on Him, sometimes salvation for others is a different recipe, one He is the master of.

Jesus is the vanilla to the batter, the chocolate chips to your grandma's famous cookies. He is the yeast that makes the bread rise, and the salt to every savory or exotic dish. There are some things we can try and "fix" and others we can fake, with the illusion we are manifesting something grand. But like cupcakes with no baking soda, or worse, no frosting, we are a flat, dull mess without Him.

So what is all this apple pie and missing belly button talk in the harsh effort of making peace with your body and achieving real wellness? I propose it is the understanding of who we are because of HIM. The world in its madness may have kicked you in your teeth a time or two, but you are adored. No matter what, no matter if this book is the best or worst thing ever written, with my dying breath, I will continue to profess: He loves you. He is for you. He is with you. He died so that you might live. He is crazy in love with you.

When did you first veer off from the perfect plan of who you were created to be? When was the first time you believed you needed to be fixed? What has been taken or added to your recipe that you know is covered by the blood of Christ? Take a moment and ponder: What parts of your story are simply dust as you peel out of the driveway? And which ones do you need Him to heal and make new?

And I will keep my word and tell you how to make the perfect apple pie, but know this, precision and planning are key. This is my apple pie; this is how I do it. Change one thing and make it yours, a sum of the whole. And call it *perfect.*

Jami's Apple Pie
6 Granny Smith apples, peeled, cut, and cubed
½ cup sugar
½ cup flour
2 tablespoons brown sugar
1 teaspoon vanilla

Mix all ingredients together until apples are well coated and pour into a prepared (uncooked) piecrust in a 9-inch, deep-dish pie pan. Prick holes in the bottom of the crust with a fork to prevent bubbling. After apples are arranged in pan, cover pie-crust edges with foil to prevent overbaking.

CRUMB TOPPING
In the bowl where apples were coated, add:
½ cup sugar
½ cup flour

½ cup butter (1 stick, cool so it will crumble well)

1 teaspoon cinnamon

1 teaspoon nutmeg

1 tablespoon brown sugar

Cut ingredients together into pea-sized crumbs and then pour/sprinkle on top of apples. Bake at 400 degrees for 10 minutes, reduce heat to 350 and continue cooking for 40 to 45 minutes. I leave the foil on for the entire time and do not remove it until the pie is slightly cooled so that the crust stays intact. Serve warm with vanilla ice cream or fresh whipped cream! Serves 6 to 8 or sometimes 2 to 4!

*For more recipes and gluten-free options, visit https://sacredgroundstickyfloors.com/category/cooking/

Well, Girl Wisdom

For a moment, consider that which makes you, you. And I want you to add nothing "bad" to the batter. The ingredients I want you to choose for the purposes of this exercise are the things you are good at. I want you to consider five things that are uniquely and positively you. And I understand, you may have a few things that are long since hidden by rejection or abuse—still, list them. Could you sing? Ice skate? Bake? Dance? Or do a backward flip off a diving board? List it. We will talk about our negative talk and the voices in our heads later. For now, I want you to focus on the good. Kindness, gentleness, orderly, artistic, you get it. If you were creating a new recipe, what would you list as important?

Freedom Gain

When we embrace our past, grieve, and rejoice in the arms of our Creator, it is easier to decipher what is for us and what is not. Our choices no longer need to be dictated by our hurts. The future is much easier to face when we know the Master who will guide us. Praise be to God!

CHAPTER SIX

Create in Me

In him we live and move and exist.
ACTS 17:28 NLT

With a thick piece of chalk in my hand, I hesitated to throw it into the bucket. The Vandals' remnants of the day were strewn about the yard. I looked down at the chalk and sunk to my knees. . . .

> *Sidewalk chalk drawings. They suggest the presence of little humans' artfully "correct" and oblivious minds.*
> *Destined to create.*
> *Shape.*
> *Draw.*
> *Imagine.*
> *And delight in the accomplishment.*
> *Without care for deadlines, the time, or the demand for cool mechanical air or harsh UV rays. Mindful of nothing but the current task at hand and the joy of something unique and new. . . "mine, his, hers. . .theirs."*
> *If I must create—let it be said of me that I did so without a nod to the praise of man. No, but that I did so that I might grow in my understanding of who I am—who I hope to become. . .*

and for no other reason than to delight in my destiny. If ever it becomes mundane, politically correct, or for the acclaim of talking heads, money, fame. . .cut off my hands. . .take every single medium—be it pencil, pen, paint, clay, chalk, or crayon. . .lock me in a room with a television and a recliner and leave me to rot.

For if it is no longer an expression of my soul—a longing to birth something new and fresh, I am as good as the dust from which I came.

She wrote on the sidewalk. . .just before dusk.

Jami 7-8-2018

Perhaps, had I never written a word, I would be a finer painter, or in rehab. If my expression of self were with needle and thread, would I have uncovered as much as I have about myself and my God? Certainly, I would like to think so, because it would be an expression of my true character. Back in that dorm room at my first writers' conference, barricaded by seasoned authors, ransoming me that I might "blog," I found it comical. When did blogging come into existence? Furthermore, how did it earn its rank as a verb? Alas, it has exposed me, strengthened me, shaped me, destroyed me, fashioned me, and set me free.

I believe this was the first step in falling in love with me and the creation intended for me by the

God of all. The moment I started writing, something changed in me. I am an obsessive personality—shocking, I know. I have always loved to create. My first associate's degree was in floral design. But I admit, I can only do one creative endeavor at a time. For years I would design lofty projects, heaven only knows how many Navajo dream catchers I fashioned, and I am Scottish Norwegian. But from one project to the next, I had an intense desire for more. I was awakened to passionate creativity. And it was life-giving to me to keep making new and better baubles and trinkets. In the fall of 2014, we came a sliver away from losing our foster care license after someone posted a picture of me with a foster baby on social media, which is an absolute no-no. Granted, it was done without malice, but I decided to get off social media as a precautionary measure. At that time, the only "writing" I did was on Facebook. A week later, the entire family was laid up with the flu. With no voice, physical or written, I asked Justin if I could borrow his laptop. In nine days I composed sixty thousand words on parenting. Life, social media, the everyday chaos of mom-life, wife-life, and barely getting by had packed down that which had already been shelved with negative feedback, low self-esteem, criticism, and most tragically, comparison. But once the noise subsided, I couldn't be stopped. Granted, the things I said were wholly inaccurate, and I would like to think I have come a long way, but I was creating something, and that creation was bringing me to a place where, for the first time in a long time, I liked me.

After a few months of research and composition, ideas kept bubbling up in me. Disenchanted with the idea of "Christian celebrity," I came to a conclusion: I didn't want to pursue nonfiction Christian women's writing. I wanted to kill people. Not in real life, but in pulp. I blocked out five hours every day, and I wrote murder mysteries that scared my husband to death and me, just a little. But fiction allowed me to speak from a place of "disconnect." I created outlandish and fascinating heroines, and I used detailed prose to elaborate that which was impossible and somehow totally plausible.

In September of 2015, I took my stories to the American Christian Fiction Writers Conference (ACFW) in Dallas, where I met with agent Jessica Kirkland. We immediately hit it off, and she took my proposals back to her room and asked to meet again the next day. I was up at dawn and rushed to meet Jessie for breakfast. Her words were hard. "I have no interest in this. But you sure are funny and real. You have a unique and authentic voice. Why don't you write nonfiction?" I reluctantly handed her my nonfiction proposal, and she said, "Girl, you need to blog."

Among the many accolades and accomplishments, there have been death threats, harsh criticism, and less-than-enthusiastic reviews. Aside from a stint in which I truly gave up on writing and made more dream catchers, I am a writer. And I believe a good one.

Those words were a long time coming. Before a single book deal, my brand was dumb blond. I was most accustomed to the self-ridicule and desperate character condemnation I dealt myself in heavy blows. Despite my parents' and family's constant profession of faith in me, the negative voices seem to be much brasher and influential.

Truly, this is a shame.

How many eyes will fall upon this page and burn with tears of remorse? Too many. For the world has smothered many a dream with its punitive criticism and damaging campaigns. Dear one, what is your passion? What can you make? What did you dream about? And who told you to stop? Or did you stop because someone told you no? Or said, "That is terrible!" Beauty is in the eye of the beholder, and you are gazed upon by the grandest of Beings. A Creator who made you in His image.

When I told Jessie, my agent and now close friend, about this chapter, she was over the moon. After seven years as a literary agent working with creatives, she assured me, "The minute a creative person stops creating their passion, they almost certainly fall into depression, bad habits, or bullying." Bullying? Really? But this makes total sense. We were created for a purpose. Dear one, no matter what you have been told or what you lie, you have made your truth; you were created for a purpose too. And when that purpose is neglected or abandoned, our spirits seek out anything to normalize. Think about the heart of a bully. They most often are discontent with something in themselves, so they victimize people around them to justify themselves or feel empowered. Maybe this is a small step in stopping the bullying epidemic: get those bad guys a brand-new box of crayons or a ukulele! Deep within us, there is a rumbling. It may manifest the very worst in us or something completely new and delightful.

I propose that we have a myriad of issues that are holding us back from a destiny intended for peace. In her book *The Art of Amen*, author and friend Catherine Bird puts it most poetically, "The birds of the sky, the fish of the sea, and the animals of the land all reflect the artistic nature of God."[2] A God whose image we were made like. Among the greatest issues in self-esteem, I stand firmly in my belief that we esteem not ourselves because we know not ourselves.

And yes, I understand we are not all writers, musicians, painters, actors, or poet laureates. But we were designed by a creative Creator to create. We were knit together with color, texture, fragrance, and movement. Furthermore, we were then given the ability to create, facilitate, build, and move. And we were fashioned with talents that then varied the depth, width, breadth, and velocity of those elements to make things even more unique and impressive.

Yet few of us follow those instincts past the eighth grade. Why is this? What breaks the natural drive to let loose and let creativity happen? Additionally, the

---

[2]Bird, Catherine. *The Art of Amen*. (Leafwood Publishers: April 9, 2019)

thing you love, that is your art. . .yes, even algebra or accounting. But are you doing it? And are you doing it well? By well, I mean, is it pleasing to you? Not long after Jessica signed to represent me as my agent, my first rejection letter came with the reasoning that I wasn't "just one thing." Meaning the publisher needed to know what my jam was. Was I a home-school mom or a displaced evangelical Catholic? Was I giving home economics advice? Or just ranting about self-absorbed dance recital moms? Who was I? And at the time, I didn't know. But what I did know was, I wasn't just one thing. And I knew I wouldn't be boxed in for the sake of book peddling. Writing had empowered me; I was systematically turning into a confident being. What would that look like for you? If you have found it, are you neck-deep or just skimming your toes in the idea?

I recall the boiling deep in my gut, a desire to prove that publisher wrong. A longing to come out swinging with all things Jami. I also remember thinking, "Wait till they get a load of me." The rejection was a clue into who I was as a creator. It was a raw reminder; I had lost myself a long time ago. It was a spark that ignited a fire in me. Rejection can do that; it can seem like the end when, in reality, it is just the beginning. It was the last straw on a camel with a broken and arthritic back. Rejection had been a catalyst in breaking me, silencing me. Then in an instant, it was the fuel to my fire. It was a paradigm shift I cannot explain, but I am forever grateful.

So what do you need to rekindle that creative being in you? Do you need to be encouraged? Or rejected? What is the thing that would make you jump out of bed and race to meet the day and make something no one else has ever made?

I offer that the stifling of our creativity is key to experiencing the freedom we need to love ourselves again. Strange? Okay, call me strange. But here I am, pounding out book three. When I started, I was at my chubbiest, in my least favorite size, and brimming with confidence and delighting in the creation of words. As I tap at the keys and search my Thesaurus for the next outstanding word, I feel empowered, brave, and alive! This is me at my very best, and I suggest you can have what I have. A reason to get out of bed in the morning. A fire in your belly that doesn't rationalize or bow to the praise of man but instead craves the next artistic download from the God of your creation.

And nope, I am not telling you to get an agent, quit your day job, or try and be her or me. What I am telling you is. . .be the *you* He intended. Start now, and see for yourself. Ask God to remind you who you are, what you wanted. Be open to something new, start making plans, believe big, and explore some options. Now, in the margins of this book. What did you want? What did you dream? What can or will you create if you have the confidence to chase it down and conquer it?

At our younger son's school, they do an end-of-the-year assembly, and the teacher lets each child walk to the mic and say what they hope to be when they grow up. This year I kept a tally: 4 firemen, 12 artists, 3 ballerinas, a nurse, 4 teachers, a policeman, and 3 ninjas. Not one of them had "no idea" or walked to the mic and said, "Well, I hope to be a news anchor, but I will probably settle for something less to pay the bills and barely get by. My marriage will most likely fail, one of my kids will go to prison, and then I will probably have to work at Circle K to pay alimony when my wife takes everything I have."

Okay, life can kick you in the teeth; we have established that. But God created you for life and life abundant. Are you choosing that life? It is a choice, you know. Or are you setting up camp in the ashes waiting for a lottery ticket to blow in your face? I have been in the throes of depression. I have been in the pit of despair and poverty, but once I found my identity in Jesus Christ and followed Him down the path of truly believing Him, not just simply acknowledging His existence, *but really believing Him*, He showed me something: a desire to create and reveal myself as accomplished. I prayed for wisdom and sat down and wrote. I didn't name it and claim it, but I said yes. And the rest has fallen into place at an exponential rate.

Does that mean I am a *New York Times* bestseller? No. (Well, not yet.) Does that mean I have a vacation house in Maui? No. Does it mean that I have been spared heartache or that I am a size 4? No. But what it does mean is that I recognize myself for the first time in my adult life. I am an author. I am an artist.

This is the craft He designed in me, and I delight in it as He delights in me (Psalm 104:31).

Stuffing Ashes and Daisies

The book you are holding was met with the breadth of rejection. But I am here to testify, while God is not the author of detriment, He will use every line of brokenness to show His glory. And while I am wholly opposed to saying, "All things work together for good!" to someone face down on the pavement of anguish, I believe He will do this.

I traveled to a spa in the woods to write a wellness book. It was a completely different book than the one you are holding. If I am to be honest, which apparently I will be, I am positive it would not have embodied the freedom I have now found. I struggled the entire week—well, struggled like you do at a spa. I mean struggle as in suburban, Americanized mama struggle and not oppressed, segregated, or starving struggle. I digress.

I took a break from my attempts and headed to the medical center on the spa campus. The treatment I would partake in was actually recommended by my doctor to balance my liver enzymes. Yeah, a colonic. Basically, instead of a massage, I would be indulging in forcible pooping. Can we not talk about this anymore?

Thanks.

Anyway, in the waiting room, a spunky blond woman arrived in a fluffy white robe, right behind me.

And while you might not believe me, I am an introvert, especially in colonic waiting rooms. Let us not talk to each other. Also, stop looking at me. But Blakely Bering makes friends wherever she goes. God bless her.

She immediately started quizzing me at light speed. "Have you ever had a colonic? I have never had one! I am nervous! Are you nervous? This is so exciting! What's your name? I am Blakely Bering."

We shook hands, and I introduced myself. Blakely was on retreat after her recent divorce. I explained I was on a writer's retreat. She gushed. I blushed. And right before I was called back for my "treatment," she explained she was an artist and art agent. I briefly mentioned that I had an Etsy shop, and I painted to escape writing. She graciously asked if we could catch up sometime; she would "love to see my art." My intestines flip-flopped. I wasn't sure I was going to need any help with bowel cleansing. Later a quick Google search would reveal Blakely Bering is a big deal. I prayed that during her purge my name was swept away with all other toxins. I did not want this brilliant woman to see my art.

Time passed, and the book I had worked so diligently on, a book I thought would bring me and others to freedom, was met only with disappointment and rejection.

Thank God.

The last straw was in the parking lot of Hobby Lobby; my agent, Jessie, gently delivered another blow. I threw up next to my SUV, and then I went inside and bought four canvases, new brushes, and paint. And I texted Blakely.

Here we are. An entirely new book in your hands. Freedom I had not known; I cannot wait for you to turn the pages. And, thanks to the God of my heart, a purging of my digestive system, and a "chance" encounter with a famous artist, by the time you read this my art will be on the shelves of major retailers throughout the United States. I know I may have said this, but creativity brings me to life because that is who I was created to be.

Oh friend, the truth of who we are, who we are meant to be, is paramount in loving ourselves and in turn, taking care of ourselves. All of those things can be used by this God whose ways are perfect. Scripture tells us to love our neighbor as we have loved ourselves (Mark 12:30–31). How is that even remotely possible when all we have is disdain for our existence? The challenge is to find that thing you love, and go for it!

Pass the Crayons

How many of you have delighted in the latest craze of Bible journaling? I am wholly convinced this is such a hit because it gave grown women their crayons back. Adult coloring books are bestsellers on Amazon for the same reason. The delight of creation we felt as children only stopped because we bought the lie we were too old for coloring books! It is therapeutic, cathartic, and at the core of who we are meant to be.

Moreover, maybe all you need to rekindle that spark is a coloring book, or maybe you are supposed to pursue publishing, speaking, or a teaching certification. Could it be that it is time to apply for a new job or for a loan to start that business you have dreamed of for so long?

I am of the firm belief that God doesn't instill desires in us to torment us but to motivate us. These ideas are born of something bigger He intended for us. One of my dearest friends, fellow author Katie M. Reid, is both talented and wise. Katie had much more experience than I. She had pursued publishing for several years. Months ago, Katie was editing my first published manuscript, *Stolen Jesus*. At the arc of the book, I fell into the message of grace and the completed work of the cross. Katie fell too.

I weep at the revelation. Within a month, Katie's book title changed from *Tightly Wound Woman* to *Made Like Martha: Good News for the Woman Who Gets Things Done*. She signed with an agent and was quickly picked up by a large publisher. It is a message of freedom. Before the truth of our identity in Jesus, Katie and I had both produced works-related works. Our books may have been fancifully written, but they were words of bondage. More stuff women needed to do to get closer to Jesus and be better. And then, when we were set free, God used our stories, our words, to set others free. Watching Katie's book success is one of my greatest delights. Knowing it is the truth of our Jesus brings me to my knees.

So yeah, maybe the dream has been postponed. But we serve a God who promises to make all things new and good (Isaiah 43:18–19). Maybe it just wasn't the right time, or the right message, or the place of freedom where He needed you to be. So ask Him. Go on. Ask Him. *Is this dream the right one? Here I am, Lord; is it time now? Where will You take me if I just say yes?* If you can't find the courage to dream, ask Him for opportunity and courage. He is waiting to go with you on a brilliantly designed ride.

I am struck with this reality: if the book I originally wrote were out in the world now, I would have missed the truth I am living. I would have never painted. I would have never gone to the woods for clarity. I would have never met Blakely.

Maya Angelou writes in her bestselling, world-acclaimed memoir, *I Know Why the Caged Bird Sings*, "Pursue the things you love doing, and then do them so well that people can't take their eyes off you."[3] As I read Angelou's book, I was stunned to learn the book tells of her sexual assault and a consequential five-year stint of being mute from guilt, shame, and trauma. The resounding gong in this composition is that we have been silenced. Our vocal cords sliced that we might halt the battle cry "GLORY!" and sojourn as slaves to the world's judgments, evaluations, and the lies of the corporate church to keep us on the straight and narrow, in bondage, the opposite of why our God died for us.

---

[3] Maya Angelou, *I Know Why the Caged Bird Sings*, 1969. https://www.goodreads.com/quotes/290210-instead-pursue-the-things-you-love-doing-and-then-do

I am encouraged to accept as true this fundamental principle in the quest for body positivity. For years, although I am a lipstick and lashes gal, I was hiding gifts and aspirations for fear of both failure and rejection. Yet, when we risk the fiascos and refutations in the quest of that which we adore, we come glaringly near the intense knowledge of what we are gifted in and who we were intended to be.

Grit, the resolve to make a change, to improve, and in the process give all acclaim to the God that gifted you with your explicit gifts, is the passion I pray is stirring in you. A new level of inspiration is rousing in me even as I say these things. I know me well enough to know He moves. He is everything. This Spirit of "go get 'em!" is more than a passing phase, a nod to the latest fad diet, or a coupon code for free shipping on a wardrobe that will temporarily reinvent. Rather, let this be an exploding out of the gate and pursuing the grand adventure He intended just for you. Furthermore, you can't stuff a singular emotion. Or as I have heard it said, you can't ride two horses with one butt. If you are binge eating because your marriage is suffering, you are also stuffing the joy that is available to you from the love of the Father. This is so huge for me. Once I unleashed the hounds of writing and painting, I was no longer stuffing down or trying to make myself feel better via the taste buds. If I was sad and I painted daisies all day, I was experiencing heartache and simultaneously finding joy in creation. My sadness might pour out onto the page or canvas, but I am living it out in real time. Yes, I am suggesting, feel all the feels.

In a nutshell, if alcohol or Twinkies drown out the pain, so too do they roll over and suffocate the joy. I pray you are inspired by this chapter. I am eager for it to reach you. As I have composed it, the tears of gratitude have been many. I still cannot always process how quickly He has fulfilled dreams I had long since forgotten. With a God this good, so profound and enthralled with everything about me, the least I can do is acknowledge He did a good thing when He created me creative. He offers you the very same. Partner now with Him on this thing; write it out. Say it out loud. Cry out for the way. He will answer you. You need only to believe.

Well, Girl Wisdom

No idea what your thing is? Go back, get back up on that third-grade stage, and when the teacher calls your name answer, "My name is_____, and when I grow up I want to be_____ _____." Roll around in the folly. Okay, so you are sixty-two, teetering on morbidly obese, and your response was "Ballerina." Then dance, love. Quench the thirst your spirit has for creative movement and expression. Buy some soft powder-pink ballet slippers, take the clothes out of your closet, and use the bar to plié. Or, if you have the means, go to the local university and enroll in a dance class, or three! Volunteer to teach basic ballet to a nursing home, or try Zumba or Barre, but no matter what. . . *dance*. What were you created to create?

Freedom Gain

Let us give thanks that we no longer need to stuff feelings. We can use our God-inspired talents to live and create freely!

CHAPTER SEVEN

Cha-ching!

*Being confident of this, that he who began
a good work in you will carry it on to
completion until the day of Christ Jesus.*
PHILIPPIANS 1:6

I can hear the criticisms and questionings now: "That's all easy for you to say, a book deal, smokin' hot hubby, and naturally curly hair. . .A-game." Okay, yes, I am writing a book; no, I am not writing it in leg warmers and a leotard. I am in fact in pajama jeans. If they are wrong, I don't want to be right. I am on this journey with you. I might be two steps ahead in one area and six or seven steps behind in another. What we cannot do is make this about anyone but ourselves and Jesus. And while the comparison is the slow death by which many a woman chokes on her demise, this is the place we are rising up against the common.

And in the self-love game, there is one aspect that I am most convinced the enemy loves to play, and that is money. Right? Who writes about money in a body image book? Me. Why? Money is not evil; the love of money, however, is. And I propose that coin is a major distraction in our quest for peace. *Cha-ching.*

Money or the lack of it in our early years is the

great unequalizer. There were the rich kids—or you were the rich kid—and the poverty-stricken, and the mere middle class. But few grown women don't have a story of want or need in childhood that hasn't followed them into adulthood. Fitting in, the right shoes, money in your pocket, or the ability to eat, or go to the movies with a gang, these are the most primitive of an American young person's needs.

Frankly, money is always a factor. Even if you have money, it is still a factor. It must be managed, spent, saved, or counted. And if you don't have it? Well, then you want it, need it, or hope and pray some will magically appear. Among believers, there is the confusion of whether to bury it, invest it, tithe it, or give it all away and simply follow Jesus.

It is a mixed bag of all the things, none of the things, and what we need, what we want, and what we should be just fine with. I stand by this: Jesus knows. He knows the desires of your heart. And if those are less than godly, greedy, or misguided, He still knows—and He is still crazy about you. In a quest to make peace with my body, nothing has been more life-giving than coming to an understanding of what it means to live under the umbrella of grace.

Thou Shalt Not?

Years ago, my husband, Justin, and I participated in a church study on living debt-free. We practiced diligently. We had our envelopes with all our monies separated out and budgeted to the penny. During this time, one of our young children woke in the middle of the night with a horrific ear infection. Fever was ravaging our little one, and we were faced with the decision of going to the emergency room, and we didn't have insurance. We emptied the envelopes, bundled our little one, and rushed to the hospital.

Hours later, we stood in the billing office with our meager funds and reeled with panic and further sickness at the balance before us. It was $835 more than we had. Hidden in the liner of my purse was our zero-balance American Express. With guilt and trepidation, we handed over our magic plastic card and then sulked away in shame. At the next meeting, we confessed our "folly." Many a head shook at the misguided practice. And then an older gentleman chimed his objections:

You did what you had to do to help your baby. Have you ever heard the story about a guy sitting on top of his house after his town was flooded? He prayed to God to save him. A rescue boat came by and said, "Hop on before the next storm comes, and you are swept away!" The guy says, "No, I am waiting for God to save me." Another boat comes, and then a helicopter; still the guy declines the help while waiting on the good Lord. The rains come again, and just as predicted, he is swept away and drowns. When he gets to the pearly gates, he says, "Lord! Why didn't You save me?" and God says,

"I sent two boats and a helicopter! Why didn't you take the help I offered you?" So it seems to me, this is the help God offered you. You can't get so caught up in man's ways that you forget to believe in God's.

Looking back, I cannot remember how we eventually paid off that particular hospital debt. There have been many ear infections, broken bones, busted radiators, and general emergencies since that predicament. However, it has long since been paid. We never missed a meal, obviously. And we have faced other traumas, had at least one slamming-door fiscal disagreement, and paced many floors with pecuniary stressors. Yet our God remains.

There are a billion methodologies, opinions, and bank accounts. Let us not forget that we are never outside of God's love; but the minute we add an ounce of law, we are no longer operating under grace (Romans 6). And what I believe separated me from truly embracing my identity as daughter was the idea that I was in trouble with God. The inkling that we have been His last straw or the weakest link is such a misguided belief within the church. And when we stumble or make a mistake, there is this perception: He is up on high waiting to deal us a harsh punishment. Have you ever felt that way? Afraid you were about to get a holy time-out because you did something wrong?

This is a truth I want you to wholly embrace.

Ready? The death of Jesus settled God's wrath (Romans 3:25–26). He is not mad. He calls you "blessed." He refers to you as a friend (John 15:15). That was the entirety of the gift of the cross. Note the term *gift*: if you pay Him back, it is a purchase, and if you earn it, it is a wage. Neither is possible, so just say yes, and take the prize. A "yes," simply confessing Jesus is Lord, is the invitation to salvation. You are welcome to say it here and now if you never have: "Jesus, I accept You as my Lord and Savior. I believe You died for me for the forgiveness of my sins. Thank You for loving me. Teach me to love You and grow in my faith. Amen." If you accepted Him long ago and are just coming to understand the message of grace, welcome. Grace is the ultimate gift. You can do nothing, outside of believing, to become more worthy or more perfect than the *yes* that accompanied His sacrifice. I know, it doesn't seem fair or make a lick of sense. But this is how He wants it. Who are we to say no?

So, you are reading this, and you have lots of money? Great! God blessed with material funds many times throughout the Bible. Now you can bless the nations! So you have no money? Okay, ask for some; otherwise, how will you bless the nations (Genesis 12:2)? But never for a minute embrace the idea that wealth equals blessed and poor equals cursed. Again, everyone has a unique story, and each of us is called to a specific relationship with the Father.

Our prayers are never wasted, and primary in

our belief in God as Father, I feel it necessary to discuss the authenticity of prayer. When I pray with our younger sons, the prayers usually include pizza, video games, and all things little boy. And I have thrown up a few vanity-laced prayers: "Jesus, please let my jeans zip. . ." and several more desperate ones, "Jesus, please keep them safe. . .*please.*" And heaven knows I have begged a financial wish or two. At the end of the day, or fiscal quarter, He is still good, and He wants you to trust Him.

I Can. . .

I am always intrigued by the extravagance by which believers toss around Philippians 4:13: "I can do all things through Christ." We apply this to our weight-loss goals and humble human strength in turning down peach cobbler, but what Paul is actually talking about is the ability to go without or have much. Both are challenges, but we have overcome because of Jesus.

Maybe you can't buy anything you want at T.J. Maxx, which really is a bummer. But you can trust Him to take care of you. Yes, there are consequences for overspending, but do not believe He can't turn that mess into a blessing, because He said He would (Romans 8:28). I know it can be a disaster, and if you come from a history of poverty and basic human need, it is not easy to switch gears and fully rely on the mystery of God. But He is a good Father. He is your source. . .really, He is. And all He asks of you is faith, and that faith counts you as righteous (Romans 4:22).

So? What does this have to do with wellness?

Glad you asked! When it comes to wellness, there are so many misconceptions and worries that I believe we can take to Him. But among the greatest fallacies I believe we have embraced is that we are in trouble for our food. For it is not what goes into a girl that makes her unclean (Matthew 15:11). Whether you pay too much for organic raspberries or you are gorging on McDonald's, Philippians 4:6–7 (NLT) reads, "Don't worry about anything; instead, pray about everything. Tell God what you need, and thank him for all he has done. Then you will experience God's peace, which exceeds anything we can understand. His peace will guard your hearts and minds as you live in Christ Jesus."

Oh, but to truly believe. To live in Christ is to not question what is enough and what is too much. It is to be content in all things and to thrive in all circumstances. This is an image that surpasses the vision of you from behind while trying on swimsuits at JCPenney. I believe dressing room mirrors are the work of the devil. But as we dissect all the things battling our peace of mind, I pray we might start to see ourselves in a new light. A light that frames us as perfected and dictates we treat ourselves with kid gloves and gentleness.

For years I counted myself worthy for denying myself. Most assuredly, a "good Christian woman" would never splurge on a designer bag or a massage! I mean, after all, there are starving people in the world. And yes, the last shall be first and the first shall be last. But what difference is it that I count myself worthy if I sacrifice when Christ already paid the ultimate sacrifice? Crazier still, I neglect to count myself blessed when He provides me with something I truly have wanted. The Word boldly tells us there is no condemnation for those of us in Christ; nonetheless, what is stirring in your spirit? Condemnation? Guilt? Selfishness? Or pride?

What are we to boast of our sacrifices? And who are we to neglect a blessing? Self-care somehow became a bad word in Christian circles; and I submit, the lack of self-care drove many a good woman over the edge. Somehow we believed the lie that pleasure was a sin. Furthermore, we have boasted of our lack as if that somehow sanctified us as holy. Shoppers, you cannot impress the God of all with your frugality any more than He might be impressed with your shoe collection. This is grace. The truth of our identity simply by our belief. You are loved. Your coupon clipping might bless your family and allow you to bless others. But Jesus is *for* you either way.

We, as daughters, must come to God with our finances as a child can come to her daddy when in need. Okay, so your daddy was less than generous or altogether absent? And now, you find yourself carrying those wounds in a pauper's wallet. Sweet sister, let us lay that wounded wallet at the foot of the cross. Right now, let us ask Him to show us the truth about our wants, needs, finances, and debts. This is not beyond Him, my love. He knows you. He created me a lover of all things sparkly. He knows I am distracted by shiny things, and He has seen the wrestling over which lipstick to purchase. Acknowledging Him as competent in that creation has brought me to a new place of gratitude and a majestic place of satisfaction.

To the same extent, we talked about food at the beginning of this section; permission and benefit are in the same camp. I can do anything; all things are permissible. But is it beneficial? Remember, this is our motivation in seeking Him. I am not justified by my envelope budget system, but I am brought great peace in knowing that we are on financially steady ground. I can sneakily open a credit account at Target and buy things without Justin's knowledge and have the "extras" I crave, but is that beneficial? Nope. I love being able to communicate openly with Justin about money. I may be tempted to buy a shiny bauble or silky blouse that is not on my list, but chief in my confidence is the peace I have in honesty and healthy boundaries.

Okay, I get it. You are in over your head with betrayal, or you are partnered with someone who manipulates with money or rules with harsh financial authority. But you are not outside of God's reach or His bounty. Ask Him for wisdom, and He will bless you with both wisdom and solution. He is the God of restoration and generosity. What keeps you from believing Him when He says He knows the plans He has for you, plans to prosper and have a future (Jeremiah 29:11)?

If Only I Had. . .

After a podcast interview with Crystal Paine of Money Saving Mom, she and I casually chatted, and she asked me about this book. When I was done explaining, Crystal said, "Oh gosh, I need that book." Crystal is intelligent, funny, and real. She has helped hundreds of thousands of women find tangible help in financial home management and, in the process, greatly blessed her family. Her books, blog, and social media accounts are a wellspring of financial help. They also overflow with her love of Jesus. When I told another friend that I asked Crystal to read the first draft of this book, the friend said, "But she's tiny!"

I know she's tiny. I sent her a T-shirt. She wears a small. Were I to meet her in person, and I tripped and fell on her, she could die. Or at least be seriously injured. She is, obviously, also on sturdy financial ground. For that very reason, I am honored that she would consider writing the foreword of this book. She is human. She still wants more Jesus, truth, and freedom, just like a chubby person with an overdrawn checking account. We see with our eyes "tiny," but we don't know what struggles another person faces. Which is an excellent testimony to our lack. We assume that money fixes everything, and it sure doesn't

...+ it doesn't fix that which He alone came to ...ne point in my following of Crystal's ... serious car accident. Her arm was broken, and ...months her followers and I witnessed her recovery. Do you suppose that anyone stopped listening to her because she broke her arm?

"Oh, I don't listen to Crystal Paine's advice anymore. She helped me cut my grocery bill in half. . .but did you hear? She broke her arm. How can you take financial advice from someone whose bones break? Tragic."

No matter what financial season you are in, if you are T-boned by a Chevy in an intersection, you can be injured. Money is necessary. Overspending or budgeting aside, we all need Jesus, and sometimes a trip to the emergency room. And people are still people. You have room in your heart for only one God.

You Sexy Thang?

This brings me to the big plans He has for you and the price of a woman. If there is an offense to be had, let it be the belief that a woman will do anything for money. I had steered clear of all things *Fifty Shades of Grey*, the popular book and movie series by British author E. L. James. I had seen the movie trailers, read a couple of online rants about the atrocity, and then moved on with my rated-PG life, never giving the *New York Times* bestselling novel a second glance. Then a few months ago I was unable to sleep and found myself channel surfing at 1:00 a.m. I landed on

a television-edited version of the popular flick, rig
about the time the main character, Christian Grey,
gives Anastasia a red sports car.

Granted, he is handsome and rich. But handsome
and rich doesn't fix clinically insane. The "clean"
version (spoiler alert, but trust me I am doing you
a favor) includes him tying the young Anastasia up,
naked, bent over, and whipping her six times, and
making her count the lashes. Swoon? Yeah. More like
gag. If this sicko were a pizza delivery guy living in his
mom's basement, we would have already called 911.

*But he bought her a car and took her on a private
plane, and there was champagne and caviar?*

Oh well then, of course, by all means. . .that makes
physical abuse totally legit.

You know what? No way. Do what you will in
your bedroom, but do not for a minute try to make
my daughters believe that monetary compensation
is any excuse for battery. And nope, like we've dis-
cussed, there is no condemnation for those in Christ.
However, answer this question: What is the benefit of this? What good comes from the belief that
money fixes crazy? Money might make the food a
little tastier, but it doesn't upgrade a pervert, who
clearly needs counseling, into a decent human being.
At one point in the "romance," and I use that term
loosely, Anastasia asks Christian Grey, "Why would
you want to hurt someone you love?"

Precisely.

In a recent lawsuit between Taylor Swift and a DJ

who groped her at a red-carpet event, a jury ruled in favor of Swift, awarding the pop star a staggering $1 in her sexual assault case against former radio DJ David Mueller. The Grammy-winning singer pursued the single-digit emblematic amount in her federal countersuit against Mueller as an opportunity to stand up for women. She testified that Mueller grabbed her bare backside during a photo op with him and his then-girlfriend Shannon Melcher, who also testified in the case. Swift's lawyer, Douglas Baldridge, said in closing arguments, "That single dollar is of immeasurable value in the scheme of things; it says *no* means *no* for all women."

And at all costs.

I cannot love this more. To heck with money, keep your hands off! And regarding dignity and worth, there should be nothing more offensive than the idea you can be bought. Of all the hurts and detriments to a woman, let us not engage or pay fancy to the notion that money is good for anything but buying groceries. For so many women, this is the offense of prostitution. The idea that we could be bought and sold for someone else's pleasure is such a tragedy. The oldest of professions, it is a misfortune that continues to destroy. Let us rally our efforts and prayers that God save the girls (and boys) that have been trafficked and grant us favor, wisdom, and intervention in stopping trafficking once and for all.

Lofty? Yep, but I am woman, hear me roar. Let us never forget, God gave us a voice.

Sex is just a red-letter issue. Our value comes from Jesus, not our partner's checking account. It is curious what goes on in the bedrooms of many. And we certainly should not get all up in our judginess. I recently learned that a long-time friend of mine was arrested for having a sexual relationship with a fifteen-year-old boy. The boy, also a mutual friend of our family, had confided (er, bragged) to his friends that their other friend's mom had sent him nude selfies and touched him inappropriately. My initial response was utter shock. I really know this person. She brought us a casserole when I was in the hospital; we had served concessions together at the state basketball championship.

My next thoughts were, *I cannot fathom sending naked pics of myself to anyone, let alone one of my son's friends. And, while I have no plans or desire to take an adulterous lover, I would like to hope I would pick someone that didn't have to be reminded to wear deodorant or entertain the argument that Cheetos aren't for breakfast.* The opinions range and rage. In some of the comments on the news article about my friend, someone said, "I doubt this boy is traumatized." Yet, I am here to tell you there'd have been a lynch mob if a man had done the same to a fifteen-year-old girl. Society's confusion about the issue of appropriateness is a battle that needs clear lines. Yes means yes, and no means no. And we cannot blur those lines for entertainment, gender, or money.

When it comes to sex, the arguments will vary.

But money, of all things, has no place in that which God created for connection, reproduction, and love. And the Good News is you were bought and paid for, not for your achievements or looks, but simply because He loves you. Knowing this to be true is a huge step in finding your whole self. And no matter your net worth, you matter.

Confidence goes so much deeper than looking like a swimsuit model. And confidence in Jesus Christ to provide, heal, reconcile, and advance you to a better place in life, marriage, finances, peace, and joy in all things is *priceless.* Oh, and by the way, He not only has endless resources and perfect solutions, but He also has perfect timing. Which brings me to the next chapter. I know, I can hardly wait either.

Well, Girl Wisdom

It is in this chapter I wanted you to look closely at what you are lacking. How long have you embraced the notion of "not enough"? Not having enough is an intense security issue rooted in fear. Lacking basic needs can lend to a spirit of insecurity and the confidence that God isn't in tune with your needs. I want to take this opportunity to call that out and ask Jesus to heal you of it. And no, this is not a prosperity gospel issue. But I would argue, for those of us in Christ, we are prospering.

Freedom Gain

You are seen. He knows. Write out your needs, hopes,

and wants. And not for another moment let us believe we are lacking. We have a Father who hears and knows us.

*For more resources on financial freedom, visit https://sacredgroundstickyfloors.com/sacred-finance.

Chapter Eight

He says, "In the time of my favor I heard you, and in the day of salvation I helped you." I tell you, now is the time of God's favor, now is the day of salvation.

2 Corinthians 6:2

What is it that sets us apart from the apes of the jungle? While many might argue worship, medicine, proper speech, or food storage, I propose it is measurement. The notes for this chapter come after a painful weekend, a weekend that marked the end of time for a young, talented, and beautiful author-colleague, Wynter Pitts. My heart races and my eyes burn at the mere thought of her passing. She was only thirty-eight, and she had only recently celebrated her fifteenth wedding anniversary and the launch of her latest book, *God's Girl Says Yes: What God Can Do When We Follow Him.*

Upon hearing of her untimely death, this is the whimper I heard most, "But she was so young," followed by, "Her babies. . .Jonathan." Death most rudely interrupts life. Our time here is short and for some of us much shorter than what we deem fair. Through my Christian author grapevine, I have heard of the tragedy too many times to count. Some stories, some rumors, others from people who were actually at the hospital and watched Wynter's family wail with the agony of time that had run out too fast.

At her funeral, which family remarkably decided to call her "Coming Home Service," it was her husband's wish that Wynter give the testimony. A large screen gave Wynter back to the world for a few moments and left us reeling with her "last words": *"I want to thank You, Lord, in advance for the perfect work You will complete in our lives and the generation of women to come."*

Timeless. Gratitude for something she could not yet see, a nod to her life's work, empowering young women, and believing in the God of all to bring that good work to completion. Something she will now witness seated with the Father, whom she lived for because she believed.

It is reported that Wynter's shocking death was the result of a heart attack. Another unbelievable variable was that Wynter was a picture of health. My mind cannot conceptualize the limited time she had on earth. And I am certain that everyone suffering this loss is struck by one particular measurement: time.

We are a clock-face-driven society. The wait is too long or too short. It happened in an instant, and we are not quite sure how it went by so fast or slow. We measure in halves, quarters, weeks, months, hours, minutes, seconds, and grading periods. We are aged.

We are dated. And we are either just in or completely out of it.

And I think it's the perfect chapter to fall before the next section as I want to encourage you. It is never too late to believe you are entirely new. By the time this book hits the shelves, Wynter will have been gone for more than two years. Ironic, she was named after a season. I will be forty-eight, and there is no telling what will have begun or ended between now and then. I am witnessing progress, but I confess, I am content either way. To have typed that and believed that is something I count among my greatest accomplishments.

I will mark it as done on a timeless list of things I had hoped to realize.

I want to take time because the message of grace is paramount in the concept of time. My sister recently relayed to me a grace-based message she heard online. And while for some it is redundant, for others, *grace* is a word they utter and a concept that evades them. They live for Christ and in total bondage to works. The message my sister shared was a basic grace message (which is hardly basic) and went like this: There were laws, things you should and should not do. Then there was Jesus. The perfect sacrifice. And He died once and for all for the forgiveness of sins. And His last words were "It is finished." He didn't come to abolish the law; He came to fulfill it. Now, nothing can separate us from Him. You cannot catch up, you cannot pay Him back. And this means you are free to just love Him and be loved.

I sat to listen to the message in its simplicity. It still slays me. The list of things to do, the ways I tried to impress Him, are for naught. Friend, my schedule blew wide open in the truth of grace. I wrote books, adopted another child, got a puppy, and sat on the porch with my husband and took deep breaths, and ceased to be panic-stricken. I scrolled to the bottom of that post to leave the comment "Hallelujah!" And there they were. The bound-up, brokenhearted, and altogether slaves to the distorted message of works-based salvation.

"Yes, but we must stop sinning."

"Agreed, but once you are saved, you must cease to do. . ."

"You cannot believe that you are wholly saved. You must work to be perfect as He was perfect."

Grace drowned out by a little work, the totality of these salvation slaves. What did it look like when there was no time left and only grace? For this, let us attend to the thief on the cross.

Calvary

The prophetic day was broken up into timeless fragments of blood, tears, terror, nudity, and humiliation. I imagine the lurch in Mary's womb. Can you feign the sensation, almost like you were falling, when your gut convulses at a terror? She observed her boy being brutalized for humanity; she had been forewarned, yet she couldn't have imagined. He was blameless and dear, and she, His mother, was helpless: unable to watch, powerless to look away. Finally, He was nailed to a ruthless piece of wood and raised to His destruction. From below, she sees Him, her baby, and He, through parched, cracked lips, offers salvation to the genuine criminals, who earned their place on torturous crosses to His right and left.

One denies Him, mocking, ignoring the ultimate gift. The other accepts Him. And He, in His gentle goodness, defines the moment: "Today, you will be with Me in paradise." There is no time left.

The thief is righteous because He believes. That is all.

He cannot climb down from the cross and pay his tithe, reconcile his debt, confess, foster or adopt orphans, deliver meals to shut-ins, build houses for the homeless, take cookies to widows, volunteer at the bake sale, wake early to read scripture, or sanctify himself in any way other than to say, "Yes, Lord."

Time is up, and he has chosen.

If there had been another option, I believe that God would have spared Jesus this brutal death. And we tell this story. Our babies know it by heart; we peered through terrified fingers as we watched it play out in the lifelike movie *The Passion of the Christ*. But I think we miss two of the most important aspects of the story. One, the act by which the thief was saved, a simple "yes." And two, "It is finished."

It Is Finished.

How much time I gained when I fell into the arms of grace. It took a while to adjust to the freedom. And now, I am certain that He has been leading me down a path to more freedom, more time gifted back to me, and exponentially increasing my freedom.

In the quest for body positivity and Beloved Living, time is most definitely a factor. Lack of it more than anything. If I had a dollar for every time I said "I don't have time," I would use the proceeds to buy more time. But a lack of time is often the culprit for the empty McDonald's sack on the dining room table or the gym bag, *still* neatly packed at the foot of my bed. Often, there is time left over to accomplish a healthy home-cooked meal or that late-afternoon cycling class, but by now, the time to rest is my focus.

Some women manage their time with precision and perfection. And then some women are a hot mess marked by tardiness and chaos, but the common thread between the two is still time. Failing to utilize our time can definitely be a factor in Beloved Living. So far, other than prayers, I have hoped not to add to your list of things to do. In my research, that is the common denominator in wellness body image books, the dreaded "you should." You should eat this, not that, and do this, not that, and here is when, why, and for how long.

Perhaps I am too rebellious, but you are not the boss of me. Stop telling me what to do; I don't have time for that. At my best, I get a full eight and a half hours of sleep. I have time alone with God before the madness starts. And I have meal plans completed, groceries bought, and the laundry caught up. Alas, time management often equates to mind management and keeps the crazy at bay. Still, it takes just one hiccup. A flat tire, a phone call from a rogue whack-a-do relative, or a kid puking, and all is lost.

As I collected data for this book, and a friend suggested I add *time* to the Beloved Living dialogue, I was undone by the revelation. My ability or lack in the management of time goes a long way in making sure I am attending to my needs as well as everyone else's and even further in the level of contentedness I take in the achievement.

Of all the factors, let us not allow this one to get away from us. Time. We must make room for it for ourselves. We must be cognizant of others. We mustn't take it for granted or take advantage. We must be alert to it but not controlled by it. We are not more or less because it is more or less. It is simply a measure by *when* we get things done.

Still, as the time has come to venture on to the next section, what I no longer want to waste is time on quick fixes, fads, or gimmicks. I want to save my time and energy not hop from one failed solution to the next. Or waste time trying to be a size society deems "good" and requires I never, ever, ever, have wedding cake again, no, not even one last time.

And I do not want to waste time on regret, but there is some. All the trends, fads, money, and emotions that go into wanting to be different, resenting those who are, and hating others we begrudge or do not understand. Might I suggest in the grand art of comparison and judgment you interject a measure of grace? He loves you just as you are. He loves them—yes, your enemies, even though you disagree with their very fiber. And it goes a long way, letting go of hate, unforgiveness, or prejudice, to remember He is their Father too.

Pastor and author John Sheasby, who was born and raised in South Africa, talks about time wasted on prejudice. After relocating to America, he began to recognize the handicap afforded him by the instilled emotion toward African American and Hispanic humans. He decided to isolate himself to pray about this. With his yellow notepad in hand, he got on his knees and asked God about this prejudice. He professes he heard God say, *"Well, if you hate them, you must hate their Creator. So, first, you need to forgive Me for creating an inferior being."*[4]

Mic drop.

I can prescribe treatment for reclaiming time, and that is to let go of every single negative feeling you have for yourself and others by wholly submitting to grace. We cannot believe that God is all-knowing and perfect and in the same mind hold on to self-hate, hate, and prejudices. He tells us in 1 John 4:20, you cannot love God and hate your brother. And friend, letting go of that hate might seem impossible; believe me, I have been there, but there is nothing impossible with God. Take back your time, take back your energy, and lay your hatred at the foot of the cross.

---

[4] John Sheasby sermon video series, https://liberatedliving.com/store/for-purchase/the-freedom-of-forgiveness/

God tells us to pray for our enemies (Matthew 5:44), and I know this is easier said than done. But I propose that simply stating, "Lord, I am praying for _____, help my unbelief, make my words true," is a step in the freedom of forgiveness. And if the enemy is you, well, there is an even harder truth. But I have started, "Lord, help me see myself as You do. Help me love myself so I can love my neighbor better." And these prayers partnered? They are timeless commodities in healing the whole heart of hate of others, hate of self, and a true proclamation of love for our God.

I think a good measure of worth to consider is the time we invest in self, others, and information about wellness. As women, it is most likely we nurture those around us. This is one of the blessings of being female: even if we are not married and do not have children, many women still find the innate longing for companionship and nurturing—even adoration for a pet is an investment of time caring for something besides ourselves.

Truly I delight in caring for those I love. However, I do this better when I have also dealt myself a decent measure of care. A long bath or an egg-white facial with a cup of my favorite coffee are sometimes all it takes to rejuvenate my natural drive to minister to those around me. Other times, I might require hours either with someone or alone to reboot. Furthermore, the time I require only increases the time I have to offer others. For you cannot give someone something you do not have.

Of caregivers and moms of little ones or special needs, and teachers, nurses, social workers, and the like, this is the unseen portion of giving of self—measured in the unseen marking of time. Giving of self for the betterment of others can fill your cup to overflowing, but as with any overflow, there is spillage, and that simply must be replenished.

Sacred Standards

For the purposes of this book, we are going to talk about life rules, regulations, specifications, even positive habits as Sacred Standards. A Sacred Standard is something you do to save time, stabilize your well-being, peace of mind, and spirit. For example, my friend Michelle puts her phone on DO NOT DISTURB when she drives. Granted, we should all be doing this, but I am using Michelle as an example. This standard is something that Michelle will not be swayed from. Her reasoning is compiled of a couple of core factors. The first is that her nephew was killed by a driver who was texting. The second is that she knows she is fully capable of glancing at her phone if it is active. She states, "I know me. If I get an alert, call, or message, I want to know what's up. I have trained myself to entirely ignore my phone until I get where I am going. It is not an issue for me because I removed the issue."

Furthermore, with her phone off, Michelle, mother of seven, either embraces the silence of an empty van—on the rare occasion she is alone—or, and brace yourself for this one, she enjoys the time in the company of her children.

In a social media–driven world, with every mommy influencer endorsing their favorite wine from the confines of their closet, this spoke to me. I enjoy my children. Time has proven to fly by. If, within the confines of my car, we can visit, listen to music, or talk about their day before they are off and gone, by all means, now is the time.

Standard-setting is easier than rulemaking and breaking. We set standards for those around us: a glass of whole milk and green beans with dinner for the children, brush your teeth, make your bed, and say your prayers. We are quite quick to implement that type of order, often leaving little time for standards we require. I propose that stepping away from media, television, phone, or otherwise, we might find some missing hours that we could apply Sacred Standards to for our betterment.

To our credit, we do have some Sacred Standards already in place. I don't need to get into the habit of brushing my teeth or having my first cup of coffee on my sun porch. Those are in place and have been to the point they are a habit. Good habits that keep my teeth healthy and my coffee consumption on point. To another degree, things we do not do can be considered Sacred Standards as well. I don't smoke. I did, and I do not want to anymore. It is my Sacred Standard not to venture down this road. Also, I never waste time trying to straighten my hair. I have weighed the effort, blowing dry, then smoothing with a hot iron, and finally stepping out into the hot Houston humidity, and *poof*, wasted time.

As we go into the things we do and do not do, I do not want to waste your time or mine. We have established, time is a precious commodity. And I don't want to get into the "you should and you shouldn't" often established in body positivity and wellness. So I will tread on the precautionary and stick to scriptural truths in the hope that we are about to encounter Him and ourselves in a whole new way. To me, there is nothing more sacred or dear than coming face-to-face with Jesus and allowing Him to show me something new and life-giving. Oh friend, He loves us so much I cannot fathom that He isn't just as eager as we are for the freedom that will come when we ask Him to show us what He sees, what He loves, and what He hopes to accomplish in us, His daughters. Well, it is time to explore how to expand, streamline, and create new and better standards that are integral pieces of maintaining and making peace with the sacred temple you spend all your time in and the Lord chooses to dwell. Time is of the essence!

Well, Girl Wisdom

Do you have any Sacred Standards you implement to utilize your time? Are there habits you have formed that you credit to your mental and physical wellness? This is the most important factor: What time are you taking from the Father to fix yourself?

What time is being wasted believing the lie that your life's goal is a tiny waist, bigger boobs, or a new and improved version of you? Trust me, moving forward, we are devoting every single second to a God who will help us streamline our time by seeking Him constantly.

Freedom Gain

Let us take a moment to give thanks to our Father in heaven. We are moving toward a newfound wellness that I am so excited about! I will never waste another minute on quick fixes or fads. The God I adore is now the only answer I will seek!

PART TWO

Full Frontal Freedom

"If the Son sets you free, you will be free indeed."
JOHN 8:36

CHAPTER NINE

The Ax Murderer's Diet

Since you died with Christ to the elemental spiritual forces of this world, why, as though you still belonged to the world, do you submit to its rules: "Do not handle! Do not taste! Do not touch!"? These rules, which have to do with things that are all destined to perish with use, are based on merely human commands and teachings.
COLOSSIANS 2:20–22

Betcha you would try the Ax Murderer's Diet. You've tried other ridiculous diets, right? We spend our nickels and dimes on things that we hope to perfect us. The myriad of products I have in my bathroom is a crime against my designer pocketbook with this super-cute embroidered Volkswagen bug on the front.

Alas. . .I am vain.

I love lipstick, perfume, diamonds, pearls, blushes, liners, highlighters, soaps, lotions, shadows, exfoliators, rehydrators, line diminishers, enhancers, minimizers, and all things aromatic, lovely, or those that give me hope of any aspect of the aforementioned.

Yes, I love shiny things.

I am easily distracted. And sure, I live a fast-paced,

distractible life. One minute I am writing a book, the next I am running kids to their next thing, the next I am fixing a financial debacle for a college-baby, then I am desperately trying to get a child's head unstuck from the Lincoln Logs canister, then painting, then crafting jewelry, and the next I am making meat loaf.

I have little time for myself, and when I do, I usually want what I want when I want it. I don't know that I would call myself selfish or just spread thin. But when and if I ever have a moment for a coherent thought, I recount my folly.

Rarely, wait. . .*never*, have I plopped into my chair and thought to myself, "Wow. Everything about my life is fantastic!"

No, I plop into my chair and think about how tight my pants are, how fleshy my upper arm is, or how jiggly I am. I lament the scraps of PB&J I finished off the Vandals' plates because that was all I had time for, that and eleven cups of coffee and a Cheez-It I found, I won't say where.

Finders keepers.

So in the moments I have all to myself, this is the mental anguish I pursue. It's more habitual than ritual and more ritual than spiritual, yet I add a spiritual aspect to it—just because eternal damnation is an excellent way to make myself feel every bit of sixty-plus pounds overweight. (Yes, the number is decreasing, stay with me.)

I revel in the ick.

Oooo! Look, I found another Cheez-It!

The Thin Eater

Let's take a look at the thin eater. That mystical beast who has never dipped their toes into the dieting world of "can't and shouldn't" and simply eats to nourish their bodies. I picture myself hiding in the bushes in fashionable camouflage, with pearls of course, watching the beast fancifully eating whatever they want, simply because they are hungry, and that is the food they crave.

Lunatics.

My husband is one of these exotic creatures. Justin is obnoxiously, naturally thin. He has no food allergies, and he is scarcely phased with food he loves. I mean he likes Mexican food and ice cream, but were I to offer him one of those things, and he wasn't hungry, he would just, brace yourself, *decline.*

Don't fret; I sleep with one eye open. I am sleeping next to a madman. Thank you for your concern. You are a good person.

Justin is oblivious to the law of "do not taste." He does not grapple with food issues; he doesn't have them. "Do not taste" doesn't apply to him.

That law is not for him.

He doesn't need it.

He doesn't think about it.

Similarly, I don't think of killing someone.

I am not an ax murderer. I never worry I am going to kill someone. That law is not for me. I have people I dislike, but I never worry that I will stab, poison, chop to bits, hang, mutilate, or shank a fellow human being.

And apart from the law, sin is dead, so there is the hyper-grace concern that having been told I can murder and Jesus will still love me, I may go postal and kill someone. However, my spirit cannot fathom. My heart is not in the business of killing. The Spirit that dwells in me, who loved us while we were still murderers and gluttons, loves us unto His death. And just as He has no desire to kill anyone, neither do I.

Furthermore, free from the law of "do not. . ." what do I want? Without the harsh condemnation I had once been accustomed to, and free from the slavery of THOU SHALT NOT, what shall I choose to eat? Let's say one of the choices is a doughnut. Justin might eat a doughnut because he is hungry, and that sounds good to him. Before this decision, which is a pretty creepy conclusion, Justin will undoubtedly choose *one plain cake doughnut*. He gives little to no thought to the consumption. That is just what he is going to eat. But unlike Justin, for me, there is an aspect of what it means to eat one doughnut or a dozen doughnuts. A woman raised in a diet culture who has run the gamut of dieting, starving, exercising, not exercising, and spending a lifetime chained to the burden of body image, that woman, doesn't *simply eat a doughnut.*

Okay, so, Jami, what does it mean for you to have a doughnut? Or six?

Heartburn.

Lethargy.

The feeling that a potato is lodged in my esophagus.

And the cream filling. . .self-loathing.

These things are of no benefit to me. The Spirit who dwells in me and wants all good for me has no craving for this food that is of no benefit. This is new. And in His wisdom, I grow in mine, and of this I am certain: no matter the law, there is never a reasonable excuse to eat a plain cake doughnut, because I am not clinically insane.

However. . .

My family and I were recently in a town that we rarely travel to. They have a famous chain doughnut shop. I mean, when in Rome, right? As we neared the establishment, I went into psycho mode. *How many doughnuts can I have? How many miles would I have to walk, uphill both ways, to undo the "damage"?* You know what, if you are here, you already know all the things I processed. I know you know.

But in the next moment of practicing Beloved Living, I felt the nudging, and I stopped and acknowledged it. Everything is permissible, but is it beneficial? The answer?

YES?!

I hadn't been to this establishment in years! I wanted to taste it! Check! And I was hungry! Check! I could not wait to taste and see freedom and feel its cushy, yeasty, sweet, delicious, round self between my greedy, sticky fingers. So, we went inside, and I picked two and reserved the right to get more if I felt it was beneficial.

Which I did not.

I cannot stand the taste of almond extract. If you struggle with "Thou shalt not kill," and I am in your sights, don't bother with cyanide. You won't get the almond-scented poison past me. And these doughnuts, which I believed were the end-all, were laced with almond extract. I literally spat it out and gagged to the point my eyes watered. Justin went to the counter to see if there was another option for me. Shockingly, they use almond extract in everything, including their chocolate frosting, another crime against humanity.

Greater, we asked if they had changed their recipe since the last time we had been there, and they explained that they had not. They had been using the same recipe since they opened in 1945. I have *always* hated almond extract. Yet, I had eaten at this doughnut shop at least three times before. Wait, not eaten; I binged or gorged myself at this doughnut shop at least three times before. But I did not taste. Which is a very important aspect in the Beloved Living lifestyle.

Eating faster doesn't negate the impact too much food has on the body. The body, created in His image, is pretty ingenious. A diet culture mentality breeds this obnoxious and manipulative monster of a girl that doesn't dine like a lady but instead rips the jugular out of a cyanide-soaked doughnut faster than a rabid honey badger. This is not who God created. This is not in His image. He is a gentleman, and I am His Beloved.

The Ax Murderer's Diet is the diet of law that you can and cannot eat. And you and I are free from the law. We chose the Ax Murderer's Diet every time we put restrictions on ourselves, equate them with our salvation, and then hide in shame when we fail. I am free from the law of DO NOT KILL. Whether I have accepted it or not, I am just as free as skinny Justin from the law of do not taste. Now that I have allowed myself the freedom of taste, I am shocked to find I have been eating some super-gross stuff.

Let me show you a little bit of the psychology behind this choice-based method. I love Coca-Cola over crushed ice. LOVE. IT. I pray out loud to Jesus, "Please, please, please, let there be Classic Coke in heaven. And, yes, please, let me have one upon arrival with extra Sonic ice." But here is the truth: I have a slower metabolism from the autoimmune disease I suffer from called Hashimoto's thyroiditis. I am hypersensitive to drinking my calories. On top of that, I have a sensitivity to cola flavoring and caramel coloring, which cause inflammation in my body. If I have a Coke, I can expect to wake the next morning with swollen joints and dull throbbing pain in my fingers, wrists, shoulders, hips, and knees.

I know that seems like reason enough not to drink Coke.

It's not.

I am like a three-year-old with 46 DD breasts and crow's-feet near my eyes. Nothing too aged, just enough to let you know I am not a teenager. I want what I want when I want it. And what do I want? I want a Coke—crisp, cold, and perfectly refreshing. For a long time after I was diagnosed with a sensitivity to cola, I was utterly obsessed with them. Sodas went from a drink I indulged in at the movies with a barrel of popcorn to a devastating obsession.

Justin was terribly concerned after months of illness and an expensive food sensitivity screening; he couldn't understand why I was still barely able to move or function. It made no sense. . .to him. I knew I was sneaking around behind his back, to my own detriment, drinking Coke.

Yeah, this is the utter wickedness of man. . .er, woman. Tell me I can't, and that is all that I want. I imagine Eve, lying on the banks of a babbling brook, naked, perfect, cellulite-free thighs, sun-kissed skin, sipping an ice-cold Coca-Cola. She has fresh fruit, Godiva chocolates, and if she just thinks about a piece of flaky crusted quiche Florentine, one magically appears. And then, she spies it.

Out of the corner of her eye is the forbidden fruit. She can't have that. She can have anything else she would like. But not that.

The simplicity of it is humiliating. Woman is marked for the ages. Hungry to be better, willing to risk it; the forbidden tastes so much sweeter.

Anything but that one thing.

And there's the itch. You can't have Coke. Here are some suggestions instead: sparkling water, iced tea, infused fruit water, coffee, maybe a smoothie with ripe berries, banana, and coconut milk.

Such dear suggestions.

Anything but a Coke.

But I want a Coke.

And the madness begins. All of a sudden, I need an alternate route: Coke Zero, maybe? Or a regular Coke and a few extra laps around the block. OH! I know, I'll add extra Epsom salts in my bath, some ibuprofen, and maybe I can get away with getting what I want when I want it. But most alarming in the scenario is this: not even an inkling of what God wants.

Yes, I am Eve.

I have everything. He is right here, wandering around the garden of plenty, delighting in my creation. And I in my folly have deemed Coke a sin, instead of weighing its benefits and detriments, and then there I am peering from behind a tree, naked and exposed, with swollen joints. . .*hiding from God.*

Heaven and earth!

What is the purple-hot madness? Well, I propose it comes from years of bad teachings about the law. Did I mention Jesus fulfilled the law? Yeah, at least once. But as I unwrapped those lies, I was left with a "Well, now what?" scenario, and I confess it was scary. What is a girl who has spent the better part of forty years believing in a justifiable faith? Greater, what the heck am I to do now with the extra pounds that do not separate me from the love of God but still leave me at risk of diseases and keep me in the plus-sized section?

Lucky girl, I am going to tell you.

Well, Girl Wisdom

Are you truly free from the law? Are you seeing what I am seeing? Girl! We are free! And I know this is a little scary. Diets, plans, and alternative routes have given us the illusion that we are in control. In an effort to stay in control, we have made up a new list of dos and don'ts separating us from grace and freedom. In the midst of that, we have added to the madness by creating dangerous, natural-appetite-intruding shortcuts, such as artificial preservatives and sweeteners. Again, there are no good or bad foods. What goes in doesn't make a girl unclean. Still, it can wreak havoc on our body, making clarity and Beloved Living harder to recognize. So would you feed a baby a spoonful of saccharine or a bottle full of MSG? Yeah, I don't see God shoveling that in my mouth. I see Him offering me the finer things, things He intended to nourish and strengthen for my enjoyment. He knew there would be truffles, pie, and frosting. What I don't believe He intended was us filling up way past the natural parameters of hunger and fullness, causing His design to be miserable and ashamed in her own skin. Furthermore, He created taste buds so we might enjoy salty, sweet, spicy, sour, and savory. No one knows you better than He does. He knows what you like, what you hate, and what you need. Have you asked Him? Go on, ask Him, "What would you feed me, your beloved?" Then ask yourself, *What you have done in the past to feign control?* Are you ready for the only answer? I am.

Freedom Gain

You are free. No longer are we guided by a law written in stone. Give God thanks now, and if you still feel the law being whispered in your ear, ask for God to wrap you in His protection. Plan A. . .the only option for me is ready to be harvested in the fertile soil of our hearts.

CHAPTER TEN

Plan A

"Surely then you will find delight in the Almighty and will lift up your face to God. You will pray to him, and he will hear you, and you will fulfill your vows. What you decide on will be done, and light will shine on your ways."
JOB 22:26–28

I know you want a plan. I understand. And we are almost there, but first, I must convey to you this plan. It is the only option for me from now on.

In this day and age, we hardly go a moment without. Our lives are like something out of *Star Trek*. We have a computer in our pockets. We can be in constant communication with anyone. We never get lost. We never misspell anything. And if we don't have something, Amazon will deliver it to our door in two days for free. Our attention is too fulfilled to pay. Somehow, amid abundance, here we are worn out from the search, ready to finally "get it," and yet we are missing something. And how can that be? It makes no sense. Still, we seek. Still, we wonder if we'll ever be satisfied, comfortable in our own skin, a peaceable people.

Years ago, in some church, in some town my

family had just moved to, we visited a new congregation. The pastor told a story of want and abundance. Although I was probably only ten years old, I have never forgotten the message. An older woman had saved her entire life to go on a cruise. She worked as a librarian at a small school. She was adored by the children. She was a fixture in her community. And although she never married or had children of her own, she had a very full life. For her sixty-fifth birthday, she took her meager savings and bought a ticket for a nine-day cruise in the French Riviera. In her suitcase, she packed two loaves of bread and a jar of peanut butter, dried apricots, cashews, and apples. She budgeted to the penny. She wanted to bring home souvenirs for her neighbor's grandchildren and something extra special for her grand-niece.

Although she believed it to be extravagant, she set aside thirty-five dollars. On the last night of the cruise, she planned to have dinner in the captain's dining room. She had a lovely time, she read on the deck, she stared at the turquoise waters, she saw a sea turtle, and when at port she would wander in and out of tiny exotic shops and beautiful museums. And for every meal, she retired to her room and nibbled on stale sandwiches and dreamed of the lobster dinner she would feast on in just a few more days. The last night of the cruise came, in some ways too soon. She dressed in a peach chiffon gown with tiny faux pearls on the bodice and sleeves. Feeling glamorous and proud, she made her way to the dining room. The room was magnificent. And the food was everything she'd hoped for. She tasted things she had only read about.

At her table, a lovely couple on their honeymoon inquired about her trip, and she told them how long she had saved for this adventure and this meal. She giggled and said, "I could barely afford all this, which is why I brought my own food. So that I could splurge on this last dinner before returning home." Her tablemates fidgeted and looked curiously at one another. She noted the awkwardness. The conversation shifted, but the woman next to her took her hand and leaned in and said, "You have been eating in your room?" Almost boastful, the little librarian said, "Well, yes! I could hardly afford to eat like this every day for nine days!" And the woman said, "But, ma'am, this is an all-inclusive cruise. Didn't you know, all of your meals were included in the ticket price?"

The moral of the story for that particular sermon was that we were missing out on the feast by only taking parts of the Gospel and not living our faith out to the fullest. It would be another thirty-three years before I truly understood how much I was missing. And now I realize there was even more of that story I had missed. I always have a plan B. In spite of the banquet before me, I err on the side of caution, just in case God isn't everything He promised He is.

Now, today, I can tell you that I have pulled my chair up to the table. I have tasted. I have seen. Matthew 6:31 comes to mind: "Do not worry, saying,

'What shall we eat?' or 'What shall we drink?' "

Friend, this plan is everything I ever hoped for, more than I could have dreamed of, that which I could not fathom. Until the scales were removed from my eyes and my bathroom, I was a slave to a false idol. Wait, false idols.

Worse still, I was lukewarm.

I propose we are a nation of lukewarm, golden calf worshipping, hard-hearted Christians. And yes, I can hear you balking. "Not me! I love Jesus." Yes, I do too. But (there it is, "I love, but. . ."). I, Jami Amerine, have had a divided heart. I have given more of myself to plans, programs, carbs, no carbs, extra carbs, points, ketosis, Jenny Craig, the hope of short-shorts, and any other thing that comes down the pike, never glancing up and asking, "Hey, Jesus, what do You think I should do?"

In this place of fix-it-yourself, get it right, and then you and Jesus will be all cozy, I have failed to love my God with all my heart, and I have stowed away in my cruise cabin, only dreaming of the bounty that was bought and paid for in a single *yes*. Plan B, the one I took the most confidence in, was the god of my heart. This lack of belief is the very definition of worshipping false gods.

Out of one side of my mouth, I have professed my belief; and out of the other, I have formulated a plan with which to cover my ample butt and solve all my problems, just in case Jesus doesn't answer. The details of my journey are very clearly written on my ticket. The Word tells us over and over who we are in Christ and the benefits of that belief. Still, we skip the fancy dinner and choke down less than the best, busying ourselves with our good works, laboring toward that which already belongs to us, His beloved daughters.

I propose in the journey of however many steps with so many babies thrown out with the bathwater, we return to the belief "I got it this time." Then, almost immediately after we murmur that thought, we realize, "Ugh, I don't got it. I am going down with this ship."

Which brings me to the Baby Ishmael Plan.

Plan B

As I recall, the first time this phenomenon occurred to me, I had limped into my desk chair to Skype with my friend Katie. We had only recently had a long-time foster love removed from our care. I was broken and weary. Katie and her family were in the throes of a hard season too. As we chatted and caught up, she said something, something perfect, and another piece of the big puzzle fell accurately into its place.

Katie said, "I know that we could do it that way, but it seems like a baby Ishmael solution."

Mic drop.

Ishmael was the son born to Abraham and Hagar, his wife's servant. Abraham and Sarah grew weary and began to doubt God would fulfill His promise to give them a son. So they took matters into their own hands (Genesis 12–25).

And I heard what Katie said.

For a few moments, I volleyed with myself to try and escape the truth. And then, the words that radiated in my ears assaulted my divided heart. And in an instant I knew: I am not truly trusting God. I have a plan B, C, D, E, and F. If He doesn't come through, if things fall completely apart, I got this.

In my busy mind, I have birthed, swaddled, fed, burped, and changed a bouncing baby Ishmael. I tend to him regularly. He is more real to me than the God I barely wait on to save me. He is the human side of hope when faith has run out of steam. I will interject: I truly believe that God doesn't need me to be obedient to bless me. Ishmael was blessed. That whole contrived, faithless, and adulterous act was acknowledged by God. He heard Ishmael's mother, Hagar; He didn't deny her.

God blesses. That is the entirety of His good nature. The issue isn't God's faithfulness, it is mine. In my mind, the only way financial situations get fixed is with lottery wins or some fantastic scenario where I give the Heimlich to a billionaire Japanese businessman at the Olive Garden, saving his life by extracting a crouton from his windpipe, and he writes me a check for a million dollars.

I run these wild thoughts through my mind and disguise them as a vivid imagination or Plan B when, in reality, it is a form of worry. And worry is a lack of faith. Planning around the worry? That's a baby Ishmael.

Baby Ishmael is a fussy baby with acid reflux, loose bowels, and a nasty case of cradle cap. He keeps me up nights, he busies my days, and he is a full-blown distraction from the true promise of my birthright . . .peace. My plans, man's plans, all the plans of the world fit with God's plans like socks on a rooster. Furthermore, what is it that we pray? What is it that we really believe? Here among the living, with our concrete paradises and nine to five, 1+1 = 2 formulas and strategies, what would we see if we stopped and gazed into the depths of the fourth dimension? The black hole where one-hundred-year-old women birth promised baby boys, seas part, giants fall, and a Hero rises from the dead?

In the best Christianese, we profess to believe, but. . .

But what?

Remember, there is no *but* in a perfect, "I love you." If there is a *but* in the love of Jesus, it is because we have put one there. And up until I encountered this freedom, Beloved Living, and Jesus as Plan A, our only source—no *but*—I absolutely lived and breathed the "but."

But Sarah

In the past, I have found it most easy to criticize Bible persons who tripped in their belief. I know many of us have been camped in the "Evil Eve" sorority.

I mean, Eve really caused us a wealth of hurt in her folly, primarily that whole mess with childbirth and PMS, followed by all of us having to get jobs. Personally, as stated before, I have come to have real empathy for Eve. I imagine she was quite curious. When I think of her, I see this boho-chic girl. In my mind's eye, she makes floral headdresses and ivy bracelets and necklaces out of berries and shells. I imagine her showing God, her "Daddy," what she had done that day with eager hopes He would lavish praise upon her for her creative genius. We girls love some positive affirmation.

I recall the day my first book arrived in real paperback form. I rushed copies to my mom and dad's house. My dad had me autograph one, and for the next several weeks every time I was at my parents' home or one of my kids had dropped into "Nana and Papa's," my dad was holding a copy. My daughter texted me weeks after the release HE'S STILL HOLDING YOUR BOOK. LOL.

More recently, the depths of my dad's pride were played out. It makes the top ten in Jami's Most Humiliating Moments, right below Naked in Walmart. (Insert cheap ploy to sell my other books.) We were vacationing as a family in Crested Butte, Colorado. My dad received a text from a friend with a vacation home nearby. The friend and several of his friends were at a local sushi joint, and they asked my dad to bring his brood by for a quick hello. It was like a receiving line at a wedding. All twenty of us filed past the table in a line, and my dad introduced us one by one.

After, as we wandered the darling mountain village, my dad said, "Jami, did you tell them you were an author?" Uh, nope. I didn't just interrupt a slew of the wealthy elite's lunch and say the words, "Hi! I am Jami Amerine, have you heard of me?" My parents have a habit of doing this for me to anyone who will listen—waitresses, bank tellers, grocery cashiers, the homeless. . . "This is our daughter Jami. She is famous!"

And every time I remind them: "If you have to tell someone a person is famous, it negates the fame." Anyway, my dad insisted we go back to the car and get copies of my book, interrupt these people's lunches again, and remind them I was an author. My beet-red cheeks burned with embarrassment. They were nothing but gracious and asked for pictures with me and the book. My dad beamed.

I know, some of your hurts and baggage might have been prompted by a less than adoring or even despicable daddy. This is not my cross to bear. But let me take this opportunity to say, I am so sorry. I see you. I cannot fathom your pain. And, by the time you close this book, I pray that hurt has been tended to by a Father who thinks you alone are the most famous, darling, and wonderful daughter that He ever created. So grand are you, He would lay down His own life so that you could live in complete freedom.

I digress. This is how I picture Eve and God. She

was the *first* Daddy's girl. She was face-to-face with this God. Still, she doubted her worth and His adoration, and she sought the means to be more. Just one bite. Then, you will know more, be more, and things will be better than they are now. "Go on, take a bite, girl, fix yourself."

Plan A was God as the only source of goodness. Plan B was Eve seeking to make things happen. The rest is history. Which brings me to Sarah, the wife of Abraham. Her body had failed her for the better part of one hundred years. I doubt her cloak didn't fit. I feel confident she wasn't staring at her reflection in a stream, questioning her thighs. Certainly, she didn't walk eight miles to a different stream because that one made her look thinner. But most definitely, she dipped her toes in self-loathing. She just wanted to be a mom. Why wouldn't this happen to her? All around her women birthed little humans effortlessly. Well, maybe not effortlessly, but they were able to conceive—a natural occurrence that evaded Sarah and the body I imagine she was continually disappointed by.

And here comes Abraham with news: "God told me we were going to have a son!" And Sarah is said to have LOL-ed. Long, I mean *long* past her birthing years, this was ludicrous to Sarah. Abraham convinced her to stay faithful, and for a moment, she felt the lurch in her belly. What if this was finally going to happen? So she decided, "OKAY! I believe that I, Sarah, an elderly woman, am going to have a son."

And she waited and waited. Just when it seemed like she was going to rest in her God's loving arms and trust, she thinks, "What if I just helped the process along?" And she contrives a plan: she will enlist the help of a surrogate. And once again, a biblical heroine steps away from Plan A and into the folly of Plan B.

Bless her.

The Hardest Part

This brings us to the hardest part of our humanity. Fully relying on God as our only source. We can't see Him. He isn't toting our accomplishments around, the proud papa. We can't witness Him telling everyone He meets how glorious we are. We have to trust and believe in that which we have not seen.

Sister, I know this is the hardest part of the faith walk. I too have read the promises of the Word made flesh. And I too have doubted, or worse, blatantly ignored those promises and come up with a way to see quick results. The stories of the less than faithful in our Bibles are not there to compose contempt. They are there as beacons of mistakes. He offered to spare us the shame, pain, and fallout of Plan Bs.

We have a ticket. It is an all-inclusive, bought-and-paid-for ride. Leave the peanut butter in the pantry; you won't even need an overnight bag. Everything you need for this trip has been provided. We just need to leave the comfort of our cruise cabin, boldly walk into the dining hall, and feast with the Father.

Look at you and your fancy pants!

Well, Girl Wisdom

Plan A is going to be our only plan. Do you believe the God who created you has a way for you to achieve total wellness? Can you fathom what it looks like to trust Him alone as the answer? Write out your concerns. Talk to Him. He knows what you are up against, and He has a custom plan to guide you.

Freedom Gain

This God, His ways are perfect! He will answer. Let us take a moment to rejoice. We will never have to seek any other solution.

CHAPTER ELEVEN

The Weigh-In

"Gather together and come; assemble, you fugitives from the nations. Ignorant are those who carry about idols of wood, who pray to gods that cannot save."
ISAIAH 45:20

❦

At this point in any wellness book, we have been told it is time to do the most dreaded of tasks: the weigh-in.

Cue the theme song from *Jaws*.

Record scratch.

Cue "Amazing Grace" with bagpipes.

I am going to ask you to weigh in, but it will not involve a scale. For the rest of this book, I am going to offer you an entirely new type of "weighing in." We are going deep; we are breaking the mold; we are cracking the candy-coated shell. On the other side, you will be joining me in the total freedom in which I have come to live, breathe, feast, love, and shop in the perfected size of my created self.

Welcome, sweet one.

If you have weight to lose, and this is the part you were most excited and curious about, I am excited for you. If you are rail thin, maybe even need to gain weight, and finally be set free from the battle-field that is your mind, I am over the moon with the revelations that we will now indulge in. And if you are a perfect weight but pay homage to the method by which you arrived, you are about to continue in your wellness, unshackled from the burden of a golden calf. My hands are shaking with delight, for this is what I sought for nearly all my years. The very first task at hand is to redefine the weigh-in.

At first, this might be very scary. If you are like me, which if you have made it this far, you probably are, the scale defines many aspects of your life. It is a measurement device by which we are validated and destroyed. My scale must believe it is servicing forty-five different women. It has weighed a woman whose weight has been up, down, stagnant, and stagger-ing. I have kicked it, called it horrific, very un-Christian names, bowed before it, jumped on and off it (with one eye open), prayed to it, and once I talked to it for over an hour about a cheesecake incident that still makes me weep. I threatened that scale with disembowelment should it ever breathe a word of that catastrophe to anyone for any reason. So far, it has been true to its silence. My scale has seen me naked from a very compromising view. And it has seen me ugly cry, while naked, like a crazy woman.

However, once I stopped to consider the impor-tance of the fancy pink glass ranking device, I realized it's golden-calf status in my life. And I am not telling you to get rid of your scale. That would be bossy and law-laced. I am asking you to ask yourself: Everything is permissible, but is it beneficial? You absolutely can weigh yourself, but if you are in any way associating the numbers on that bathroom scale with your worth as daughter, it is time to ask God to weigh in on the subject.

Weigh-In

The term *weigh-in* came to me in a flash. The acronym followed later. All of my Plan Bs and all of the times I cried out to God for help were glaringly obvious in that instant. I was filling pages with what my husband calls my "writer's download." Basically, I sit and "word vomit" all the things that are going on in my busy brain. And no, this type of purging has not afforded me weight loss. And yes, I have checked. My goal at that point was to come up with the plan, a plan to set me and you free from this struggle. I had just written out the words, "*False god: all the authorities I follow and create in the hopes of success, never stopping to ask Him what I should do.*" And my phone rang.

It was my doctor.

I had gone in earlier that day to pick up a prescription refill and have some blood drawn. While I was there, the nurse took my blood pressure. She asked me if I was upset or stressed. I shrugged and said, "I mean, I have six kids, a book to write, and ninety-nine loads of laundry." She wrote something down and took my blood pressure again. Of all the numbers I know to the nearest decimal point, I know nothing about blood pressure. And now, my doctor, who had been notified by the nurse, was calling to tell me my blood pressure was "dangerously high" at 143/90. Two numbers that mysteriously seemed appealing to me. She said, "I will be in touch when your lab tests come in. In the meantime, no stimulants or heavy cardio. Switch to decaf. I will get back to you."

Switch to decaf? Obviously, this woman was a monster. Then again, she just validated my excuse for skipping the gym that morning.

I returned to the download. *"False god: all the authorities I follow and create in the hopes of success, never stopping to ask Him what I should do."* And I decided to practice what I was about to preach. "Hey Jesus, it's me, what's up with my blood pressure?" I can't say I heard Him; but all of a sudden, I knew. I was taking too much thyroid hormone.

Two days later, this was confirmed. I was taking 145 mg of Natural Thyroid compound. The doctor explained, "Since you have lost so much weight, I suspect that you are overmedicated." Granted, I couldn't get past the "You have lost so much weight" statement, so I worshipped there for a little bit. And then she said, "I am cutting you to 35 mg a day. Stay in touch with me." And that quickly sent me to crazy Jami land.

Thirty-five mg a day?! I was freaking out. Why? Because, yes, at that point, I was at risk of a stroke or heart attack, but I was down two pants sizes!

You're not going to want to mess with my meds if it means I have to go buy new jeans. But I stopped and *Weighed In*.

"Hey, Jesus, I want You to be my everything. I want You to be my only option. It terrifies me to think that Beloved Living is not the reason for my current successes. Instead, my faith is weak. I am afraid to lower my dosage of thyroid medication. Help me help my unbelief. Also, please don't let me die from hypertension. Amen."

And I surrendered. Which is what I am going to ask you to do. In the process, you will want to align your heart with He who saves, which means there is going to be some golden calf crushing.

I have come to see how very little I involved Him in my life. I talked the talk. But I didn't dance the dance. And friend, it is a party.

The Weigh-In is to check in with God for basically everything. The most important part of this journey is to make God your only god. I created this acronym to help us redefine the Weigh-In.

And since its inception, I have said this prayer or reminder hundreds of times a day. It has

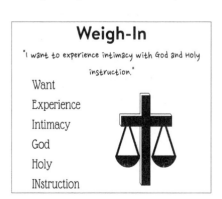

Weigh-In

"I want to experience intimacy with God and Holy instruction."

Want
Experience
Intimacy
God
Holy
INstruction

become a Sacred Standard, like brushing my teeth or wearing my seatbelt. I have lost weight. But greater, I have come to know this God whose ways are perfect, and I have ceased to be a lukewarm Christian with a divided heart.

I am happy to report He is exactly who He says He is and His promises are there for the taking. Which brings us to the lions' den.

Daniel

Daniel the prophet would not be swayed. He knew too much. He believed so deeply there was no other God before the God who drenched him in peace. He had been forbidden to pray to this God. This was not even an option. Daniel held fast to the God of His heart to his own detriment. Which was totally cool with him. And so the story goes, he was arrested for praying and led to his impending demise (Daniel 6).

We can assume it was dark, and it smelled like a neglected litter box. One might wonder, was Daniel's faith—faith that had granted him legend status in the pages of the most important Book ever written—so great his heart didn't even race at the thought? Or, as I have come to understand, was he so confident in what would happen next, he just sat on a cold rock and waited out the night? Alone with his God and giant predatory cats, I imagine he lay down and fell peacefully asleep. Perhaps a beast came over and sniffed him. Maybe another lapped its sandpaper-like tongue over his bearded cheek. But none would dine on this beloved servant of the God of Israel.

Through the ages, Daniel would be known for his faith and survival. Survival that makes no sense in the world of flesh-eating lions. Okay, I am no Daniel either. Which is the great thing about the Word of God. The Word shows us that Jesus, God who became man, had questions too. He boldly asks God why. And when others asked, He boldly answered them.

Help My Unbelief

Nothing can be as terrifying as watching the near death of a child. Whether you are a mother or not, losing someone you adore is scary and painful. In Mark 9:23–25, Jesus comes face-to-face with a father whose son is about to expire. Like Daniel, Jesus—God in the flesh—is this man's Plan A, his only hope. And he asks Jesus to help him. He begs Jesus to intervene. And Jesus says, "You got it; all you need to do is believe." To which the man replies, "I do! I do believe! Please, help my unbelief!" I can't say this is my favorite scripture, but it is in the top five. For me, it is permission to ask for more.

I am no Daniel.

I like to eat, but I have no interest in being eaten. The first time my dad traveled to Africa for a safari, we jested with him, "Don't get eaten by a lion!" He laughed and said, "I am not ready to die. But it would be a great story."

Hard pass.

But I propose we are slowly being devoured by

dozens of things, things that God had no intention of consuming us. And we feast in contempt for our belly rolls and failures and then count those follies against ourselves, furthering us from the ease of a life lived well, communing with the Father who adores us.

And He not only adores us, but He is also big enough to handle our questions. Even Jesus, His only Son, begged Him to spare Him and change the plan (Luke 22:42). And we hear no mention of God's wrath at the inquisition. He *heard* Jesus. He knew the road was impossibly scary and hard. And this is a testament to any good relationship. . .raw honesty. In the months leading up to this chapter, I have had my doubts. Dang! I even had a book contract that bound me to my thesis! And I have said, "Um, hey, God, it's me again. Although I want to lose weight and get to know You better, I also don't want to be sued by Barbour Books because the nudging of my heart was way off, and we are all supposed to be eating a 1x1-inch square of corn bread with fat-free margarine for dinner for the rest of our lives. Amen."

Again, no wrath.

No harm.

No foul.

Paramount to Weighing In, *seek Him first*. Yes, seek Him first, the kingdom of God, and His righteousness; and all these things shall be added unto you (Matthew 6:33). Which brings me to this gem: we are all going to focus on gaining instead of losing. I know it is getting weird up in here.

Gaining

It is entirely possible to change your mind about Weighing In and Gaining (Romans 12:2). Here is where the psychology of weight loss and our grand creation come into play. Of the emails I receive from readers, some of the harshest have come from those who believe that I am embracing a New Age philosophy. This started when I did a Facebook Live talk about the book *The Power of Positive Thinking* by Norman Vincent Peale.

The audiobook, a gift from my mother, is hands down one of the most important works I have ever encountered. Dr. Peale suggests that we are systematically destroying the good life offered to believers by embracing a negative outlook on every aspect of our lives. I can justly speak on Dr. Peale's behalf, the man loved Jesus. Given the opportunity, this book can offer a classic wealth of hope and a new mind. And it is biblically sound. In my studies, I have never found a scripture reference that encourages believers to talk to themselves or others about how horrible their lives are.

On the contrary, we are specifically told to focus on the positive. Philippians 4:8 states: "Finally, brothers and sisters, whatever is true, whatever is noble, whatever is right, whatever is pure, whatever is lovely, whatever is admirable—if anything is excellent or praiseworthy—think about such things." And within this scripture is embedded word after word about the power of belief. So I am forced to ask if there is power in belief, and if I believe in only failure, struggle, and a miserable existence, what will I create with that power?

Furthermore, so many of the accusers of the New Age panic are the same people lined up to buy books and teachings on the very thing to which they take offense—a Plan B that empowers their motives, neglecting the God of their creation. Not to mention the fact, the offense lends to negative thinking, dwelling on the opposite of excellent and praiseworthy, creating yet another pompous law, which looks an awful lot like a golden calf and bathing in fear, which was cast out by perfect love (1 John 4:18).

Dang, I love the download. This God, His ways are perfect (Psalm 18:30).

We are wonderfully and perfectly made (Psalm 139:14). Within that perfect design, there is a factor that allows us to think. And those thoughts speak to our bodies. If you touch a hot stove, your brain tells your body to take your hand off the heat source and do it right now. Seriously, take your hand off the stove. So then, if in our minds we tell our bodies, "Hey, I am going to punish you by not allowing you to eat real food. I am going to restrict your consumption. And in the process, I am going to tell you how much I hate you," our bodies respond in kind.

"What's that you say? Restricted calories? Uh. . . okay. Let me hold on to this fat for you. You will need it later. You're welcome."

By shifting our minds to that of gain instead of loss, we are creating inner mind space that speaks to our bodies in a language of plenty and love. I have come to believe that fat is not an enemy. That doesn't mean I want to keep it. But it was created for my benefit. Originally, the design was simply a storage system for seasons of famine so we wouldn't die when there were no buffalo. However, I have gained fat in times of little to no appetite, barely eating anything. Looking back on a season of unreasonable fat gain, I had just put my oldest son on a bus to marine boot camp and buckled our two-year-old foster love into her car seat one last time. In another season, I had a son using drugs, I was caring for my dying mother-in-law, and I had torn my calf muscle and plantar fasciitis. In that season, I was probably only eating about four hundred calories a day. I gained thirty pounds.

To which I now say to my body, thank you. Thank you for your perfect design. Thank you for wrapping me in this protective layer. Bless you, you are indeed wonderfully and perfectly made. You do exactly what you were created to do—cover this soul with armor to face the elements. Wrapping me in fleshy protection while I navigate a fallen world full of hurt and loss. Well done, friend.

So I created a new way of journaling my wellness journey. Not by what I lost but what I gained. First, I went to my favorite consignment store: I bought a blouse that was one size too small, a new ninety-nine-cent spiral notebook, and some reward stickers that said stuff like, "YOU GO GIRL!" and "GREAT JOB!" In that book, every evening, I would list what I had gained. I gained when I implemented the Weigh-In method, making every decision to the Lord. And I would gain when I went to a new dance class or kept my cool when I had every right to lose it. I wrote out and spoke kindly to myself about the accomplishments. Then I gave the accomplishments pretty little sticker trophies. And I told myself I was doing a great job in the care and keep of my God's beloved daughter. I was rocking Beloved Living. And about two weeks into the project, I gained a new blouse. One that did not fit me when I sought to be set free.

If you are a mom, this practice might make more sense; if you are not a mom and you can picture a child you love or care about, dwell on that little human. If you have to think of an animal, but for a moment imagine that innocent spirit and how you talk to them. The outcome of abuse is not pretty. The damage is substantial. And yet, this is how so many of us treat the vessel we have been gifted by a Father who loves us. We speak with contempt and ugliness. We starve and beat our bodies into submission, and we expect these vessels to respond positively? It goes against every reasonable response.

Abuse and neglect breed brokenness and want. Love and care breed wholeness and fulfillment. It seems almost ludicrous to have to say this. But I am talking to me, not just you. There is no one in my life that I would treat as harshly as I treat myself. If anyone were as cruel to one of my children as I have been to me, they would need a prosthetic limb by the time I got finished with them.

Saying it here is profound: I have a master's degree in counseling and human development. I am a certified foster parent. I know that negative talk is soul-crushing, and yet, I have justified it as a means to make my body behave. In no other instance would I use these methods to curb or change behaviors. Beloved Living is the care and keeping of a child of God. You and me. Jesus said, "It would be better for them to be thrown into the sea with a millstone tied around their neck than to cause one of these *little ones* to stumble" (Luke 17:2, emphasis added).

Little one, stop being mean to His baby. . .*you*.

Well, Girl Wisdom

Can you imagine being so confident, so in love and committed to God, that a lions' den was the equivalent to a long night in a crummy hotel? If your heart were no longer divided and YOUR Creator was your only help, do you believe you would be entirely well? If you had a billion dollars, who would you pay to direct your wellness choices? Guess what? You have the ultimate personal trainer available to change, protect, and guide. And it is free, bought and paid for with the blood of Jesus.

Freedom Gain

To Weigh In is to seek God in everything. From

now on, we will Weigh In, our Plan A, and record our gains instead of our losses. We are developing a brand-new mind, and our entire person will never be the same. Take a moment and read Ephesians 4:23–25. Then celebrate; the answer to our struggle to change was there all along.

CHAPTER TWELVE

Believe Beloved

*"Therefore I tell you, whatever you ask for in prayer,
believe that you have received it, and it will be yours."*
MARK 11:24

About two years before I would fall headlong into the arms of the real Jesus and the message of grace, our family was faced with the looming removal of our first foster placement, a baby boy who had been in our care for nearly a year and a half. It was a dark and scary place. Paramount to my fears, knowing he would not be safe, I grieved for what he would think. We had wholly bonded and delighted in each other. When I would walk into the room, he would audibly belly laugh. In spite of that deep connection and even though his birth family had not met any of the requirements for his safe return, in forty-eight hours his caseworker would be coming to pick him up and deliver him into a home he had not known.

I was tormented with the thought of the baby boy wondering where I had gone. In my grief and worry, all resources exhausted, an acquaintance who heard of our struggle invited me to come to her church for a prayer/healing service. Although I was soaking up every last moment of my time as this boy's mommy, I decided that after I put him to sleep, I would go to the service.

I arrived a little after 9 p.m. The woman who invited me was not there, but another woman who had been alerted to my situation by my acquaintance found me and took me to a room where there were several people quietly sitting in folding chairs, writing on forms attached to clipboards. The woman gave me the same. She explained to me that I needed to fill out the form, and she would come and get me shortly.

I still have that form.

I poured my heart out, fear and brokenness, so much misplaced hatred for myself. And so much confusion about the God who died to save me. I didn't understand the injustice of what was about to happen to our family or the baby we believed belonged with us. One line reads, "If I have done something wrong, PLEASE, show me how to fix it." At the bottom of the page were lines to list my sins. One of those lines read "GLUTTON."

I waited and wept.

Shortly after that, the woman came to retrieve me. She explained to me that my acquaintance had informed the prayer team of our dire situation. I would be prayed for by their "best" intercessor. And this part is hard for me. You don't have to believe in this sort of thing to benefit from the message. Until now, other than the confidence of one friend, I have never told anyone about what happened next.

My escort opened the door. A slim, older gentleman and a stunning redhead were seated in two of the three chairs in a circle. The redhead stood and smiled adoringly at me. The man and I made eye contact, and he gasped and put his face in his hands and sobbed.

I never even sat down. The other women were entirely shocked. The man stood and walked over to me, put his hands on my head, and began to pray. It was short. "Jesus, she does not know how much You love her. She doesn't believe. Help her unbelief." He removed his hands from my head, moved them to my shoulders, and said, "You don't belong here. You have everything you need. Go and believe."

And I left.

The next day my acquaintance called and apologized that I hadn't had a more positive experience and expanded. "That man is usually so helpful. I don't know what that was all about." At the time, I didn't either. Whether it is right or wrong—and face it, we have all met with questions about doctrine, theologies, and the mysteries of the Holy Spirit—I believe that man was spot-on about me.

I didn't understand. I didn't believe.

What I thought about Jesus then was that He was a works-based God. Many times I have referred to Him as the If/Then Jesus. The concept is mandatory in comprehending grace. It is the belief that if we do something right or wrong, then God will move one way or the other. I am fully convinced this belief system keeps us separated from a God with arms open wide. At that moment, I believed that the baby boy in my care was being removed from our home because I was a lazy glutton. If I hadn't eaten those Cheez-Its, if I had made it to the gym seven days a week, and if I was a better, size 4 human, God would bless us with custody of this boy. Sister, that god is a monster with no gauge of good and evil.

That is not my God.

Under the cloak of that death-breeding belief, good and decent human beings, church-going, tithe-paying, charitable, and devout believers are being dealt with cancer, financial hardship, and untimely deaths. They are convinced, "God must be trying to teach them something." And if that is not the work of the enemy to infiltrate the church, I do not know what is.

In the simplest of terms, if God moved because we were good or bad, then the cross was wasted. He died for us while we still sinned. We cannot earn or pay back the sacrifice of the cross. If God is for us, then who can be against us (Romans 8:31)?

And while sin is sin is sin, in the scope of child safety, we were hands down the better choice—Cheez-Its eating included—than the choice the courts were making for that baby. Jesus said, "I have told you these things, so that in me you may have peace. In this world you will have trouble. But take heart! I have overcome the world" (John 16:33).

And with only hours to go before the caseworker would arrive, there was nothing left to do but surrender and believe.

I ate Cheez-Its and packed the little boy's clothes. The rest is miraculous history.

My good and bad works were not the motives for the eventual adoption of Charlie—the little foster boy who was nearly removed—into our lives forever. Likewise, God was not the author of the heartbreak that came two years later when our foster daughter returned to her birth family after two years in our care. He was with us as we cared for that little girl. He held us close as we grieved her removal. And He has never left us.

Our belief counts us righteous (Romans 4:24). It is counterintuitive to sit in ashes and profess His contempt. It goes against everything that He paid for our freedom.

Say it with me: "I am His Beloved."

Girl, Save Yourself

Amid bad theology, women around the world are desperate to finally get it. I am here to testify, we have not because we ask not (James 4:2). Maybe that makes no sense. We are asking, right? Well, I propose we are asking the wrong authority. If we are to remain lukewarm with our hearts divided, we have not fully stepped into the dining hall of freedom.

So at the persuading of my literary agent, I listened to a bestselling "self-help" book on audio while driving to and from my oldest son's wedding. My agent was not encouraging me to listen to the book because she believed I needed the message. Instead, she wanted me to listen so that I might understand her frustration with the popular message.

And, I am not here to debate good and bad books with you. I am here to make a point about Beloved Living, that which is for me and that which is not. Also, we are individuals who will grow by different means. I enjoyed parts of this particular book. The author is articulate and funny. We actually have some stuff in common. But at one point, I was forced to pull over and sob. As the author spoke of her book's successes, I was forced to acknowledge I had not met with that kind of success. She made it sound so simple. And she was suggesting that success could be achieved with a "can do" attitude.

However, I am not a professional marketer, and I am not married to a wealthy, professional marketer. I fell into the world of publishing nearly by accident. I had none of the connections or resources this author had when she was first published. But her message is that a lack of success is directly tied to a lack of belief in *yourself*. I can promise, I have believed in myself and my Plan Bs above all else. I blew my nose, dried my eyes, offered my books back to Jesus, and drove on.

And then she talked about the loss of her foster placements. This I could identify with. Until she talked about her family now. Her testimony was that she would not give up on the dream of adopting a little girl. And she has that little girl. She believed in herself and her dreams, and now she has a beautiful baby girl.

I pulled into a Sonic drive-in, lay my head on the steering wheel, and grieved.

Our adoption journey began with a dream of a little girl. I would not trade Sam and Charlie's placement in our lives for all the money in the world. They are my sons. However, only weeks before our son's wedding, trying to convince Justin we should pursue foster care and adoption one more time, my husband's answer to my plea "I just knew we would have a daughter. . ." was "We did, we do."

We had a baby girl in our care. We poured into her and her mother. We sacrificed emotionally and financially. We loved well. While we do not get to raise that little girl, she will always be our daughter.

When I was done weeping for my loss, my grief turned to those women who might hear this message of manifesting blessings based on our tenacity and spunk. Women who have buried a child. Daughters of my good and loving God whose arms ache for the blessing of a child and remain childless. Sisters who are widowed, broke, chronically ill, run-down, worn out, and ready to give up. What about them?

It was then that I was struck with the significant importance of Beloved Living. No matter what disappointments you face, you are adored. You matter. There is this space where we speak truth and positivity into our lives because Jesus said to. And there is another space where life is going to deal us some seemingly impossible situations. It is in that place where I propose that surrender, without a doubt that God is still good, is the safest place to find sanctuary.

There will always be some teaching that is placed before us that seems new and fresh. I am not above admitting to coveting the successes of another author and speaker. I know my struggles. But their story is not my story. And while I am certain if we met, I would hug your neck and we might be fast friends, there is a part of me that can't help but hope these words set you free, and you never give me a second thought. I am not the answer.

I have been fan-girl myself. It is easy to fall under the spell of the rich and famous. When someone in authority directs you in a good teaching that advances you, it's easy to pay homage to that person and hold them in a place of honor. However, there is room in our hearts for only one God. Beloved Living means embracing the truth of who God is and how much He loves you. He is for you and with you. He is for your health and well-being. Were His motives anything else, the cross makes no sense. It would have been the brutal slaying of a God for the show.

The cross is everything. It is not just part of salvation—it is *all* of salvation.

The Diet Altar

As I mentioned above, it is very easy to esteem that which has helped us. I have been there. Right now,

I am bombarded with news of the latest successes from the current diet craze. It won't be the first or last bandwagon. But I am committed to never jumping on again; that commitment has become a Sacred Standard. I won't go back.

I was recently invited to join a social media group singing the praises of a diet. I hopped on because that has been my reaction to a new diet for thirty-three years; old habits die hard. But I quickly left and grieved the insanity. Friend, no matter how God leads you individually in your quest for wellness, you cannot serve two masters. You will love one and hate the other (Matthew 6:24).

And it reminded me, years ago while traveling, Justin and I stopped at his favorite barbecue spot. They serve slabs of meat on butcher paper. The seating is picnic tables, so you sit with strangers to eat. And because it is so popular, you are elbow to elbow with everyone and their cousins. We were seated with three women. They were your average Texas buxom broads, big hair, thick accents, and huge purses. One of them pulled a one-pound block of cheese out of her purse. The other two inquired, "Is that part of your new diet?" She boasted, "Yes! I can eat this pork chop and brisket and this block of cheese!"

No, sweetie, you cannot.

Actually, I was wrong. Because she did. And here is where I witnessed the wreckage of the diet altar. When she was finished eating a pound of everything, she was still hungry. And her friends were able to convince her to have some cobbler with them. I am not judging her; I have had my share of food follies. But many of them began with a new diet and ended with a heart that never got full.

Hungry hearts are driven to teachings where you can have more of everything. Again, there are no good and bad foods. What goes into a girl doesn't make her unclean. But it sure can keep her slave to outlandish, albeit misunderstood, teachings. We were created to crave. And she won't get anywhere in her health pursuits by eating copious amounts of food of one kind and then relying on willpower not to chase it with cobbler.

I didn't know it then. As a matter of fact, I leaned in closer to hear what the eating plan was. But these diets lord over us and make us more unhappy, more hungry, than we were when we started.

I cannot speak for you. But as for me and my "house," we will only serve the Living God (Joshua 24:15). I am not saying this to you with an ounce of piety: I have walked away from concepts of any salvation other than Jesus. I do not want to serve any other God. I do not want to be lukewarm. And I no longer wish to battle the world when it was already overcome (John 16:33).

Your convictions or needs are uniquely yours. You may not be able to swallow a bite of anything with a face or a mother. And you might benefit from a low-carb lifestyle. Sugar might make you crazy, and gluten might chain you to the potty for weeks at a time.

But there is only one Savior. He is the way, the truth, and the life (John 14:6). He is the answer.

I really like Him.

And He is crazy about me. And madly in love with you.

Go on, believe.

Well, Girl Wisdom

I have tried to save myself. Had I been successful, this book would just be another book to lead you down another path, another Plan B that may or may not work for an individual daughter with an individual story, that cannot save you from yourself. What Plan Bs have you tried? How have they kept you shackled? Are you ready to surrender?

Freedom Gain

Take a moment to give thanks that you won't need any other plan. Your belief sets you apart and counts you well.

CHAPTER THIRTEEN

Taste and See Wisdom

If any of you lacks wisdom, you should ask God,
who gives generously to all without finding
fault, and it will be given to you.
JAMES 1:5

*I*f you are still here and didn't jump ship because we don't like the same books, this chapter is everything to me. And I want to start from a place where we can agree to disagree, simply because of wisdom and good old-fashioned common sense. However, for the purpose of this book, common sense is being kicked to the curb, and we are now going to be referring to "Spirit Sense." Face it, common sense can evade some of us from time to time, which I will continue to prove. Also, I am an expert in the fall of common sense. Not so much as I have lost it, but more because I have six children, four of whom are sons. In my journey as a mother, I would say that common sense fails sons more often than daughters by a ten to one ratio. I witness a lack of common sense daily.

Again, I am not into male bashing. At the same time, I have never had to take one of my girls to the emergency room to have her head removed from an object in which it was lodged, multiple times.

Still, where the mind is common and easily infiltrated, the Holy Spirit is the guardian and chief authority of the senses. The mind needs to scooch on over.

I had a stunning revelation. It was hard to dissect. Earlier in this book I prayed I would be able to make you see all that is before us. I mean, why did you pick up this book? Probably for the same reason we read any nonfiction personal-growth book. We crave answers. But it now occurs to me that was not the correct plea. Within my prose, the answers for you, an individual daughter of the Most High, are different than the answers for me. The truth of who we are and what we need are categorically unique. God, in His infinite wisdom, created us with an exclusive design. Still, we seek the same "plan" without regard for that one-of-a-kind thumbprint. Common sense tells me not to touch a hot stove, but did you know there is a disease that prevents people from feeling pain? The afflicted have to be constantly monitored to protect them from hot stoves because their brain doesn't tell them it is hot.

Beloved Living, seeking all the answers from He who created us, is rooted in our individual needs. This is entirely delightful. It means that instead of law following, written in stone, for the world which was overcome, I get to meet with my Creator and be led by the Spirit. If sense were common, none of us would have a single internal struggle. And we would not be able to logically justify the death and resurrection of Jesus.

As believers, we err on the side of nonsensical all the time. Yet, while we say we believe in Him, our minds constantly remind us of the impossible. Simultaneously, we let outside forces dictate what is for us and what is not. The crisis, or stall-out in our progress, lends to who we allow to dictate what we think instead of asking what He might have in mind for our well-being and restoration.

NO-maste

Years ago, I was the director of wellness at a YMCA. Among my duties was to teach several aerobics classes. On Tuesdays and Thursdays, I taught yoga. And because it was a Christian establishment and fitness yoga is not a religious practice, I did not use the traditional language of yoga. I was not encouraging anyone to breathe into their third eye, and I wasn't aligning chakras or talking to dead Hindus. *That is not for me.* And in gyms across the nation, millions of people are incorporating *fitness yoga* into their workout routines.

One day after teaching a water aerobics class, a woman came into the dressing room looking for me. I was alerted to her presence by the sound of her shuffle. She was nearly crippled from back pain, walking with the aid of a walker. I had seen her before in water aerobics. But today she donned stretchy pants (solidarity) and a T-shirt.

She introduced herself and proceeded to tell me that she was no longer able to attend water aerobics. Her back was so badly injured, simply getting in and out of the pool and her swimsuit was debilitating. She wanted to know about my yoga class. Her doctor, a family friend of mine, had told her about my class. She was desperate.

With the help of her doctor, she began attending my yoga class. The goal was to strengthen her abdominal muscles to support her back and hopefully heal her young body.

In the first class, she barely moved. But for every pose she could not accomplish, she would engage her core and breathe. Two weeks later, she could almost touch her toes. Two months later, she had said goodbye to her walker. And six months later, she was able to follow along with the class, and she was doing thirty minutes on the treadmill after that. Over the moon, with her life back, she lost twenty-two pounds.

And then one Tuesday she didn't show up to class. She was in my office when I finished teaching. She handed me a card, canceling her membership. She could barely speak; she was so sad. She explained to me that her pastor found out she was taking yoga classes. He had shown up to her house the night before with an elder from their church to confront her. He told her that the practice was endangering her salvation. . .(*Nothing* can separate you from the love of Jesus; it is literally in the Bible. I am not making that up). And that she must stop taking the classes and repent.

I did my very best to convince her that he was misinformed. I pleaded with her: "I will call him myself and explain it. He can come and participate for free!" I didn't even end the class with "Namaste," the traditional closing of a yoga practice, which roughly means, "I bow to you, you bow to me." No offense, I am not bowing to you, don't bow to me. Okay? Alas, she could not be swayed.

Granted, she could have continued exercising, and while I am not condemning her in any way, she had met the goal of strengthening her core. This too could have been maintained in other ways. But she not only did not ever come back to yoga, six months later I saw her in the grocery store in a wheelchair. I use this as an example of how often common sense evades us and, more importantly, how we allow outside forces to dictate that which might benefit us.

When I started taking yoga classes at the same YMCA where I would come to teach, I too was injured. The stretching and toning granted me swift gains and led to a season where I delighted in helping others and supplemented our income. Looking back, I can see where I was blessed by the work. And I can also see where I ignored common sense, ending that season, but not soon enough.

Not for You, Jami

About a year after that encounter, the new director of the YMCA, who was a menace to society, wreaked havoc on the establishment. He was a predator who groped and sexually harassed my colleagues and me. In turn, I was very short on aerobics instructors. Under atrocious conditions, including verbal lashings that went so far as hour-long, screaming phone calls to our homes, employees began jumping ship.

One morning I taught two back-to-back cycling classes and two back-to-back water aerobics classes. Utterly depleted, I limped to my office. The director barked at me from down the hall, "The kickboxing instructor quit. It's a full house, go teach it!" I said, "I don't know how to teach kickboxing." He charged at me and yelled, "FIGURE IT OUT! We don't cancel classes!" Then he looked me up and down and said, "And don't hire any more fat aerobics instructors." And pinched the back of my arm.

I know.

I know what I should have said. In my mind, I clearly heard, "Jami, this is over. It is not worth it."

The voice followed me to the class, where twenty-plus students waited for a qualified instructor to teach them kickboxing. I heard the voice again, "Jami, don't."

But Jami did.

And ten minutes into the class, I was hobbled. I felt the pain in my soul. Four hours later an emergency room doctor informed me that I had torn my calf muscle and ligaments in the arch of my foot.

A week later, I resigned.

A couple of months later, I was called to testify in

an ethics hearing for the director. He would later be fired, although they declined to have him drawn and quartered, a more appropriate consequence, in my opinion.

It is pretty easy to neglect common sense. Spirit sense, when I am truly communing with Jesus, well, I have found Him much harder to deny.

The Helper

Time and again, I come across scripture that I have memorized and have neglected. More often than not, I have added a "but" to scripture to validate my wretchedness. Nothing can separate you from the love of God, but wow, that was bad. Go to your room.

Nothing can separate you from the love of God. . . **but.** There is no *but.* And by no means does this mean we are continuing something that is not for us (Romans 6:2). So while the mind and what we might justify as common sense might encourage us to do something that is wholly against God's goodwill, the Holy Spirit will not lead us astray.

The flesh is a pesky being, which is the reason Jesus sent the Holy Spirit, our Helper. What I am compelled to point out is this: it is outlandish to believe in a man being raised from the dead, but it is laughable to believe that mystery and neglect every other aspect of the gift. Truly, if He was raised from the dead three days later, why do we doubt that He is capable of every other single thing in the world?

The greatest mystery, Christ in you, the hope of glory (Colossians 1:27). . .but I don't know what to do next? My struggles volley for brain space. There is the common science of calories in and calories out. And if one were to teach twenty-six aerobics classes in a week, one might consider themselves quite the fitness guru. Still, seemingly strong, articulate, even highly educated women with voices, opinions, and convictions negate the power of Christ and follow blindly behind the world and its promises right into the belly of the beast.

Yes, God can turn ashes into beauty (Isaiah 61:3). And He can make all things work together for good (Romans 8:28). But imagine how much free time He would have for you if instead of cleaning up the messes, He alone took you around them.

What I cannot do is look back and wish for what I did not know. Once again, if not for the valley, there would be no summit. However, I hope to never be so dull as to make those mistakes again. Common sense, the world and its ways pick at me to pick a diet plan so that I might finally be free of the roller coaster. I hate roller coasters.

Spirit Sense, the Helper I was promised, continually shows me the world's answers are not always His answers. Holy Spirit wisdom is wholly apart from the mind. To taste and see wisdom, holy, ordained wisdom, is where I now rest. And friend, I was tired.

Scripture states the Spirit's presence is shown in

some way *in each person* for the good of all (1 Corinthians 12:7). If you have ever traveled outside of the United States or even to a large city, like New York or Chicago, this might resonate a bit more. Never have I felt as small and insignificant as I did the first time I left the country. On a balcony in Caracas, Venezuela, I wept at the very idea that He who calls me by name can possibly keep track of all these humans. Common sense would say no way. Spirit Sense says, *"Yes, Jami. I knew you before you were knit together in secret"* (Psalm 139:13). *"I know the plans I have for you. Plans to prosper you and not to harm you, plans to give you hope and a future"* (Jeremiah 29:11). *"Ask, and it will be given to you; seek and you will find; knock and the door will be opened"* (Matthew 7:7). And *"I am leaving you a Helper to guide you in wisdom and save you in times of distress"* (John 14:25–27).

I will stress what the Holy Spirit guides me in might be a polar opposite from what He offers you. Neither of us will be led by the Holy Spirit to sin. . . ever. So I enlisted the help of a friend in testing the waters of Beloved Living. She suffered from diabetes and needed to lose 150 pounds. At every turn, she was met with the benefits of a low-carb lifestyle. Seeing her rapid success, I was tempted to follow her example. However, I am not a big meat eater. For reasons that I will not disclose because I want you to follow Him—not me, my wisdom, wisdom the

Holy Spirit poured into me, proved that path was not for me.

And four months into my friend's journey, wisdom prompted her to add a little fruit back into her diet. Her weight continues to drop. She Weighs In with Him constantly. Her *Gains*, in her love and trust of the Holy Spirit, are most significant. That friend has this scripture posted all over her home and car: "In the same way the Spirit also comes to help us, weak as we are. For we do not know how we ought to pray; the Spirit himself pleads with God for us in groans that words cannot express" (Romans 8:26 GNT). He alone has saved her. He is her only plan, Plan A. She feasts with the Father, who grants her wisdom and rescues her in her time of need. Beloved Living is her norm.

Beloved, dig in, wisdom is yours for the taking.

Well, Girl Wisdom

Where common sense and the flesh collide, God pours out the Holy Spirit abundantly on us through Jesus Christ, our Savior (Titus 3:6). And because of this wisdom, I can no longer wander the desert in search of any other answer. Are you guided by the flesh or His Spirit?

Freedom Gain

It is time! We are nearly there, and while this journey will not rest until we are face-to-face with the

Father, the most exciting part is that He is our only answer now! Let us give thanks and worship! The Spirit will never take us where we don't belong, and we can trust Him to keep us where we are safe!

CHAPTER FOURTEEN

Sacred Sweat (Don't Panic)

*So whether you eat or drink or whatever
you do, do it all for the glory of God.*
1 CORINTHIANS 10:31

You can assume I exercise and like it. Assume nothing. Perhaps I used to be quite the athlete. But years of abuse, coupled with years of neglect, have left me pretty much stationary. But this is probably for the best as I dive or slowly meander into this chapter at a comfortable pace. I would like to think this will come as a comfort to some. Especially if you are chronically ill or just really prone to napping. There are plenty of books written by plenty of taut, fit wonder women touting their accomplishments and the stellar results of this workout or that. You go, girls! If you delight in the activity and you are not law-bound, good for you. Honestly, I am delighted you have found balance and something that you love.

I am a healthy, strong person. Perhaps not as strong as I was when I was training for a half marathon or teaching an obscene amount of aerobics classes. But I can carry a week's worth of groceries into the house in one trip. And I can open a jar of pickles all by myself. For the purposes of this book, I am completely content to come before you and testify exercise has been a blessing and a curse.

The blessing comes from the intricate design God created in me to move. I say that with trepidation, for I know eyes might fall on this that are confined to a wheelchair or debilitated by fibromyalgia, or a wealth of other physical struggles. And if that is you, hello sister. I see you. I have felt the pangs of immobility. I am so sorry for your suffering. Jesus knows you; He loves you. You matter.

The exercise curse was obviously self-induced. And I abused my body and tormented my mind with the have-tos and shaming shoulds.

In one of those seasons, I was forced to vacate the gym and partake in physical therapy. I am fascinated by physical therapy. In mere days of starting a recovery program, patients see the results of rebuilding and strengthening body parts that are not functioning at full capacity. Like the women from my yoga class, gaining muscle has grand benefits.

And, as is the recurring theme of this book, I cannot tell you what you should do to move your body. I am not your keeper. While I can testify to the benefits of a regular exercise routine, it is a slippery slope between law and freedom.

One day we are told we need to exercise three days a week for thirty minutes. The next day science changes. You need only 10 minutes of high-intensity interval training (HIIT). Yoga might be for one, while others might believe yoga will land them in their basement with a Ouija board. I get it. I also know navigating the world of exercise is like trying to paint the moon. Who can possibly know what madness will erupt next? Have you heard of goat yoga? This is a real thing. Goats climb on you while you maintain a downward-facing dog.

In Beloved Living, I needn't consult the Holy Spirit in the validity of goat yoga for me. But if you like it and are so inclined. . .well, have at it, girl.

The hardest thing I have encountered in my exercise routine is not allowing movement to become my baby Ishmael. Just like I am prone to worship at the altar of Weight Watcher points, so too am I inclined to build an altar to CrossFit or Spin classes. A divided heart, false gods, and golden calves suddenly sneak into my life, strong-arming the gentle God and nesting in His seat.

Most recently, while I was regularly attending to exercise, I broke my tailbone. In classic Jami mode, I decided to move my desk closer to the window in my office. And yes, I heard the voice, "Hey Jami, go get Justin to help you."

I am a hard study.

As I pulled the heavy antique desk across the room, walking backward, I tripped over a power strip and landed on a steel electrical box in the middle of the floor. I blacked out from the pain. Once I was able to regain my wits, my first thought was, *Oh dear. I am terribly injured.* The second thought, *Great. . .there goes my new workout routine. Hello, fatty.*

Oh Jami, but if you are not so very hard on His girl.

While I have experienced many an injury— seriously, this book makes me sound like a poorly trained stunt woman—what I see is a woman who is wholly committed to her Plan Bs. At every turn, I have supplemented or replaced God's goodwill and safekeeping with anything to aid in the process.

Yes, exercise is good for me. It keeps my heart healthy and my muscles toned. However, were I to never walk another mile, God loves me. To believe I am made righteous by my fitness is to believe I can earn His favor by strength and endurance. I am happy to report that this is not accurate.

So, I came to this chapter, knowing that I needed some training, but it would be a new type of training. And while I have physically trained my body like a professional prizefighter, this type of training was harder than any I had ever encountered, but I never broke a sweat. I needed to train my mind to rethink exercise and move it from an idol to an act of worship.

Weighed Down

This is not the first time I entertained the idea of inviting God into the arena of my health and wellness pursuits. Yeah, I talked to Him in yoga class, and actually when I go to yoga now I talk to Him still. But as a young mother of our only child at the time,

Maggie, I was desperate to lose twenty pounds of "baby weight." Consumed with the process, I was sweat deep in a two-hour elliptical session, listening to a radio program on my Walkman. (Wow, that was archaic.) The radio program host was breaking down the formula for calories in and calories out. This narrator was explaining how to reach the perfect heart rate and balance that with the exact minutes maintained to lose one pound. His words attacked me.

"Anything else will NEVER work. Don't even bother."

I stopped peddling. The elliptical machine lowered me to the ground slowly. I wiped down the machine and hit the showers. As I scrubbed the sweat from my body, salty tears and sweat washed down the drain, along with my hope. I really hate math, but that wasn't the reason for my breakdown. The fact was, I couldn't keep up with any other thing that precisely. And I deeply swallowed contempt and failure.

I was drowning in my newfound motherhood, home management, graduate studies, no sleep, and my schedule at the university teaching freshman seminar and psychology. Adding to that a preoccupation with numbers that truly were a mystery and would not save me from myself, this broke my heart and added to my burden.

I got dressed, grabbed Maggie from the nursery, and ate my way through the heartbreak, thus adding back the ten pounds I had lost in the weeks before the meltdown. The only book or teaching I could identify with was Eric Carle's *The Very Hungry Caterpillar*. Most nights, I was too tired to finish reading it.

And then one Sunday at church they announced a new Bible study for weight loss. I fully believed it was an answer to prayer. Honestly, in some ways it was. I now see the dangers of law-based teaching and the interference those teachings play in Beloved Living. The majority of the study was darling. The love of God, food freedom, and there were no requirements to exercise unless you enjoyed it. I lost all of my baby weight at an exponential rate. But as the study and new way progressed, red flags flew high all around me. I kept my head low, worshipped the founder of the study, and stepped farther away from the truth of who I was in Jesus Christ.

The law of this study was to only eat when you were hungry and stop when you are full. Fair enough, that is a good practice. Second, only eat half of every portion, saving the rest for the next time your stomach growled. Okay. That makes sense. After all, portion sizes in the United States are pretty hefty. And third, do not mess this up or you will meet with the wrath of God so intensely you will never make it to the sidewalk leading up to the pearly gates. Shame and condemnation followed. It was all kinds of ugly.

If I thought I was a wreck that day on the elliptical when I thought I was going to have to do actual math, the belief that God hated me left me entirely destroyed. And what did Eve do when she thought God hated her for her disobedience?

That's right, she hid.

Justified by works is the most bitter form of belief. It stays thick on the tongue, and it pours forth gallons of ugliness. Self-righteousness is ugly. Self-loathing is morbid. Believing in a god who hates us is utterly horrifying. I choked on my confusion, and then I ran and hid. Unable to keep up with His imaginary demands on my life and behavior, I would spend the next years confusing His will with teachings and plans that were not for me.

Years later, exhausted and sore from teaching dozens of aerobics classes over just three days, I went to the mall to buy a new outfit for a dinner that my husband and I were supposed to attend. The salesclerk handed pants to me over the dressing room door. I had started with a size 12, perhaps out of habit. She continued to retrieve smaller sizes. The last, which fit like a glove, was a size 4.

I stood in disbelief, this waif of a girl, in a tiny size, heartbroken and miserable. The clerk inquired if I was okay or if I needed her to get me a size 2. I cleared my throat and dismissed her and sat on the floor and, once again, wept. What I knew for certain was that I could not keep this up. Besides being physically spent, I was starving to death. I was legit hungry. But I was also spiritually famished.

The exercise and low-caloric regime could not be maintained, but more importantly, I could not face the terror of a god who demanded perfection and condemned my every deed. With mascara-stained cheeks, I left the mall without making a purchase. It would be many years and many more plans and pounds before I would fall into the arms of the Real Jesus.

Work-ship

I believe that exercise is important in living a Beloved Life. Among the many theologies I have embraced, there is a common theme, and yes, it does come from scripture. "Do you not know that your bodies are temples of the Holy Spirit, who is in you, whom you have received from God? You are not your own" (1 Corinthians 6:19). And I believe that. What I can no longer embrace or believe is that that scripture is a threat. I think a lot of people believe that it is.

It is a fire and brimstone teaching. You better, *or else.*

God doesn't make mistakes. I want to ask Him why He took the long way around the horn with Adam and Eve. I cannot fathom that He did not know that Eve would stumble at the tree of good and evil. But she did. The only answer was Jesus. Still, we go back to the tree, looking for scraps of what to do to earn back the pleasure of His company.

The enemy slithers about, he whispers Plan Bs, ways to be better and do better, little suggestions to be more perfect. He is slick if nothing else. Every time we step away from living as the Beloved Chosen, our eyes are wholly focused on what Satan has to offer, the perfect distraction.

There is no harm in adoring a particular workout. We were created for pleasure. Why else would we have been blessed with the senses? Taste, touch, smell, and sight drench us in His goodness. However, as a species that craves indulgences, I can't help but believe those senses are something He hoped we would trust Him with.

Instead of gifting ourselves the pleasure of building muscles, rocking it out in an aerobic dance class, and then replenishing our bodies with wholesome and tasty foods (i.e., watermelon—which is straight from Jesus), we count ourselves righteous by pushing those muscles past their limits, questioning the godliness of dance, and washing down the misguided feats with a powdered whey shake with a shelf life of one hundred years.

So while I was redefining the Weigh-In, it occurred to me: the best way to change my mind about exercise was to do the same thing. A workout as worship. In my humanness, I have deemed worship as only an act of hand-holding and praise-singing to be done on Sundays and Wednesday nights in a particular building at an exact time. Yet another gift I have neglected or deformed.

In Katie M. Reid's book, *Made Like Martha*, guest contributor Nicole Homan writes, "Worship is simply loving God back."[5] And this spoke to me in a whole

---

[5] Katie M. Reid, *Made Like Martha: Good News for the Woman Who Gets Things Done* (New York: Waterbrook, 2018), 31.

new way. What more could I possibly offer to the One who died for me, that I love? I could tell you any number of ways to work out; heaven knows, I have tried all of them, except for goat yoga. Seriously, I am not doing that (stop bringing it up).

I have seen and experienced the power of a well-trained body. However, whether your body is bikini-ready or morbidly out of whack, if you have not embraced the freely given love of God, peace will be what you chase. And even if you can run a seven-minute mile, it will evade you. I promise.

All we truly have to offer Him is worship. And I am eager to do this. Not because I have to but because I want to. I want to celebrate Him. I want everything I do to be a translation of my love. And so, I stopped working out and started *worshipping out.* It might seem like sleight of hand, but obviously, I am pretty easily duped. I would Weigh In, "Hey, Jesus, help me choose a workout today, one that honors this temple where You dwell. And one that allows me to worship You through movement."

I confess, as someone who worked out for a living for years, some of His suggestions were quite "fluffy." I went to a beginner tap dance class, and while I cannot say that my shuffle-ball-toe would prepare me for a marathon, it was quite fun. Another time I attended a yoga class near my home that was the equivalent of a nap. And yes, I would start to question Him, "Hey, it's me again, is this of benefit?" The resounding gong? *"Yes, sweet girl, rest."* And I lay on my mat and whispered, "I love You, Jesus. . . ," until I woke myself up snoring. The next day I was led to a very hard but super fun Nia dance class, complete with praise and worship music. And the next day, He tested my limits.

No Sudden Movements

I began the day by Weighing In. In my journal, I wrote out the names of readers who had messaged me prayer requests. And then I wrote some scriptures that popped in my head. I placed the day before Him and asked for wisdom in all my decisions and circumstances. Next, I wrote WORKOUT? I doodled little barbells and firecrackers around the word. I opened the app on my phone that tells me the workout schedule at my gym. There was not a single class available that would fit within my busy day.

And I went into panic mode.

I said it out loud. "HEY! I NEED TO KNOW WHAT TO DO! REMEMBER! THIS IS ME! WEIGHING IN!"

Nothing.

And I thought, well, if God wasn't going to show me, I would just do it myself.

And here is the fine line, no other gods before this God whose ways are perfect. I was being invited to rest. But an exercise-obsessed Jami is a girl steeped in legalism. Legalism is an idol.

I did some Lamaze breathing. I wrote in my journal, "I am afraid that if I miss a day, I won't get back to the gym *ever* again." And I sat with that. Then, I grabbed a pink marker and fancifully wrote "Perfect love drives out fear" (1 John 4:18). Again I spoke out loud. "I am not afraid to miss a workout. I can worship You in my car after I drop the Vandals. This isn't the first or last day at the gym. Thank You, Lord, for this day of rest."

And I closed my journal and went about a day of Beloved Living.

Peace Out

I am most cognizant of this: exercise is not the answer to wellness. Yes, you can train the body and reap the benefits. But to be truly well, we must be peace-filled. I was not peace-filled on an elliptical with baby fat to lose. And I was not peace-filled in a dressing room wearing size 4 slacks. I regularly exercise now, and I would say that exercise is a Sacred Standard for me. I need to move. When I don't, I don't sleep well. And I suffer from restless leg syndrome, which started after I had Sophie. Exercise lessens these symptoms.

Exercise affords me benefits, but I propose, especially if you are unable to exercise or have not incorporated it into your Beloved Lifestyle, you can still have peace. Furthermore, if you Weigh In and you require movement, you will know it is time, and you will know what exercise you will benefit from.

Rage on, girl!

Well, Girl Wisdom

Tap into the power offered you through Christ, our Lord, and ask Him to show you. Ask Him how much, how long, and what He wants for you. There is no better personal trainer on the planet than the Father who created you to move. What movement do you love? How can you worship Him with movement?

Freedom Gains

This God, oh how I love Him! I no longer have to be a slave to the elliptical. Let us thank Him for the freedom of never "have to" and always "Can't wait to love you back!"

CHAPTER FIFTEEN

The Making of a Princess

Therefore you are no longer a slave, but a [daughter];
and if a [daughter], then an heir through God.
GALATIANS 4:7 NASB

Once upon a time, there was a beautiful and successful actress. She had left an abusive marriage and rebuilt her life in Hollywood. She had a lucrative career and a voice for women's issues. Of biracial descent, the young actress was a beacon of light for many minority women. She championed the causes. And then she met a handsome redheaded prince from a foreign land. They laughed and talked and became very good friends. The friendship evolved, and the couple fell in love and married.

The marriage granted the actress a new title, one of nobility. She would leave America and her career and join her new husband's royal family. Her life would never be the same. She would never drive herself anywhere again. She couldn't go to Starbucks or Target—pause for a moment of silence. But the love she had for her new husband was worth being something entirely new.

And unless you are living under a rock or locked

in a basement, being held against your will, you know I am talking about the marriage of actress Meghan Markle and Prince Harry, grandson of Queen Elizabeth II of the United Kingdom. Granted, since I first wrote this, she and her prince have "resigned" from their official royal status, but the point is still valid. And I am left to wonder, the morning after the wedding, if she started her day by trying to convince herself she is now really who the world says she is. I would guess not.

I can't fathom Meghan has to mechanically list the things that make her "royalty." Granted, she might have to pinch herself now and again to make sure she is not dreaming. And while someone is fixing her food, and servants tend to her every beck and call, and she never has to ever check her bank balance at an ATM, that is not what defines her as the Duchess of Sussex. The reality of who she is now is because of love. The greatest gift and commandment has afforded her many a little girl's dreams.

In a doctor's office I read an article in the waiting room about Meghan Markle's shoes. The article, which was a year old at the time, contained magnified pictures of Meghan's shoes, which were all, obviously, one size too big. Many people were inquiring as to why she would have shoes that did not fit. The answer? Well, she was in "princess feet training."

Meghan's royal stylist was training Meghan's feet to withstand 4-inch stilettos. She was teaching her feet to stand in hours-long receiving lines and walk upstairs in glamorous, expensive, sleek heels. Meghan was strengthening her feet and ankles and was learning how to move about with grace and elegance in impossible shoes. A fashion reporter explained, she needs the extra room in a larger shoe to prevent blisters and accommodate for swelling as she grows accustomed to these shoes.

I know, poor little lamb.

But I was struck by this. She is a member of the royal family. You can't argue her life has been undeniably changed forever. Still, there is some work to be done.

The Lighthearted Life

No doubt Meghan Markle won life's lottery. And while she had to sacrifice her home, social media accounts, and career, love was worth it. Well, love and the newfound luxurious lifestyle probably eases the struggle. The young woman beams with delight. Since this chapter was first scripted, the newlyweds welcomed a son. They are obviously deliriously happy. At the same time, the media is quick to report the ongoing battle Meghan has with her birth father.

Meghan's father has sold stories and pictures of his daughter to tabloids and disparaged her in public. This man, her own father, didn't come to the royal wedding. Prince Charles, Meghan's new father-in-law, walked her down the aisle. Similarly in a recent interview, Meghan's husband, Prince Harry, was asked about the death of his mother, Princess Diana, in 1997. Visibly saddened by the story, he conveyed the detriment of his mother's untimely death. With devout admiration, Harry talks about the common girl who became the People's Princess. He voices how much he wishes he could have introduced his bride and son to his mother and what a wonderful "grandmum" Diana would have been.

The Duke and Duchess of Sussex (their formal royal title) are full-on royalty. But they still carry the wounds of the world. Still, I would bet Meghan's journal does not read, "Meghan, you are nobility, don't forget to act like it." Her life manifests all the perks of royalty.

I propose ours does too.

No, a limo is not coming to pick you up. And I would discourage you from buying the shoes Meghan is wearing. But the ease of her life as royalty comes from embracing who she is now. There is no battle to stay in the present or change her mind about her new role. She faces no internal battle for her reality. And, we, the daughters of the King, have been invited to a life free from worry and striving.

Yet we kick off our heels and wander to the servants' quarters to dine on doubt. Here is where we must do the work of princess living. I am going to do it in flip-flops; you can wear whichever shoes you would like. From this point forward, we are going to think like a princess.

This is the most lighthearted aspect of Beloved Living. Even if you lack in any area of your life, there is one thing that has helped me above all others: "My grace is sufficient" (2 Corinthians 12:9). I might have some grief. And I may meet with an impossible situation. But I take ease in those trials because I know who I am, and I know the God that fashioned me.

Easy street.

Becoming a Princess Picky Eater

Remember the story of "The Princess and the Pea"? A queen wants to find the perfect princess to marry the heir to the throne. The queen decides to test the candidates by their frail comforts. She puts a pea under a stack of mattresses. The next morning she asks her guests how they slept. Each time the young, would-be bride reports how she slept. The winner of the prince's hand is the girl that did not sleep well because of the tiny lump in the mattress.

This is the mindset I am suggesting for a food plan. So elegant and accustomed to the good life are you. You could hardly sleep on a lumpy mattress, let alone eat from a trash can.

But it is less "What would Meghan Markle eat?" and more "What is the king offering me?" First, a member of nobility has manners. With all eyes on her, I have found no reports of Meghan inhaling a cheeseburger and wiping her mouth on her sleeve. She eats small bites; she has a napkin in her lap. Eating is intentional, slow, and elegant.

Yes, I had six minutes to eat lunch yesterday, but I

used every bit of that six minutes to

1. Weigh In (I want to experience God and Holy Instruction)
2. Sit down
3. Pray over my food
4. Feast with the Father
   a. Put my food down between bites and clear my pallet with a drink
   b. Chew with my mouth closed and use my napkin
   c. Smell, taste, feel, and see my food
   d. Stop when I am full

If you are a serial dieter, you have heard some or all of these suggestions before. Chew your food, don't eat after seven, eat nine times a day, eat one time a day, eat no carbs, eat no fat, eat all the fat, eat all the carbs, never skip breakfast, never eat breakfast, eat this, not that, and never, ever, ever...

You know.

However, I believe the reason the above formula has worked for me is that I Weigh In with Him, giving Him thanks and eating satisfying, *real* food I love, the way He created me. This leaves me spiritually fed and physically satisfied. And physical satisfaction is important in achieving and maintaining a healthy weight. But to be full-on communing with Jesus leaves me fully satisfied.

The more I have leaned into Him and His plans for me, the less food I have needed or wanted. Face it, we do not want to suffer. And it is no fun to be hungry when God created us to eat. But when our hearts are empty or hurting, biologically all we know to do is seek comfort. So, we eat. And in doing so, we produce hormones that offer us pleasure. That is why funeral potlucks taste so good. We need something.

To the same degree, if we are suffering and under the law of do not taste, our brains set off alarm bells. We create a battlefield of the mind. Feel better, but you can't have that, do not taste. And the stress hormones go nuts. The spiritual struggle is against our very creation. Which is where stopping to Weigh In and say to Jesus, "This is what I am feeling. This is what I want for comfort. How would You guide me?"

Okay. Hear me out. If you have ever wanted what you want and considered prayerfully asking God for help, I know you will identify with this. "I don't want to ask Him. I just want a Reese's Peanut Butter Cup!" Been there. Eaten the cup. Have the T-shirt. And scripture tells us, "No temptation has overtaken you except what is common to mankind. And God is faithful; he will not let you be tempted beyond what you can bear. But when you are tempted, he will also provide a way out so that you can endure it" (1 Corinthians 10:13).

The caveat is, you don't want to escape, you want a Reese's Cup!

However, once your entire heart is feasting with the Father, this becomes less of a struggle. I recently met with such an incident. I didn't want to escape. But more than those instincts, I could not bring myself to say, "Hey, Jesus, I don't want You to be a part of these next few minutes. Go away. I will get back to You when I am desperate and full."

Ugh.

Spirit-Fullness

There is nothing new under the sun. The type of cognizant eating suggested above is most commonly referred to as intuitive or mindful eating. But my mind is never empty, which is probably what makes me an authority on the subject. I recently returned from a writers' getaway. I was gone for five days. When I pulled in the driveway, Sam and Charlie came running out to greet me and help me with my things. In the chaos Sam's head got shut in the door, leaving a huge goose egg. About an hour later, I came to check on him, and he said, "My head sometimes gets ahead of me, and then I gots nuffin but trouble."

Precisely.

My mind, the things I have believed about myself, food, nutrition, and wellness have caused me nothing but trouble. I can't trust my mind to fully protect me from the elements, obviously. But the Holy Spirit can be fully trusted. I believe that 1 Corinthians 10:13 is a beautiful promise of how God will rescue us. We must believe in who we are in Christ and let the Word dwell in us, turning away from any other answer. Jesus is the key to feasting with the Father. After a season of Weighing In, saying "I want to experience intimacy with God, holy instruction" will trump the desperate need to eat when you are feeling something other than hunger.

The struggle within comes from years of a divided heart. And this creates in us a last supper mentality.

The Last Supper

No, not that last supper. The one time (or hundreds of times) you decide to go outside the natural instincts of hunger and fullness and make promises that are destined to fail. Face it, to never have chips and salsa EVER AGAIN is not from Jesus. And there are no good and bad foods unless, of course, you are allergic to chips and salsa. If you are, I am so sorry. I hope you are getting counseling.

But the internal dialogue of *never again* leads to overconsumption. Which happens even to naturally thin people. The difference is a naturally thin eater might eat a lot of chips and salsa. And then they won't eat again until they are hungry. And when they eat when they are hungry, they eat what they want, and they stop when they are full. Their body knows it can trust that thin person to feed it, and feed it well, the next time it needs it. The naturally thin eater's body is not continually releasing panic hormones, convincing it there are no more buffalo, because eating is not a crisis.

Mic drop. *Eating is not a crisis.* It is just a meal. It might be incredibly delicious. It might just be a bowl of Cheerios. But it is simply a gift from God, enough nutrition at that moment.

And yes, you might have a lot of weight to lose. You might not be able to tolerate certain foods. Your doctor might ask you to try a specific diet or incorporate something into your personal path to wellness, but by Weighing In with God in everything, even that is going to be fine as long as it never takes His place on the throne of your heart.

How He Saves

There has been this misguided perception by Christians that depression is a manifestation of a lack of faith. In the composition of this book, I met with a season of depression myself. And my doctor gave me a prescription for a mild antidepressant. I Weighed In. Jesus and I talked about this a lot before I took a single dose. In my heart, I knew that I not only needed this medication to get over the hump, I knew that Jesus was totally cool with it. Just like I mentioned earlier, His gentle nudging had me convinced that I was taking too much thyroid medication.

My stress hormones had been on high alert for more than three years. Book publishing and speaking gigs had left me depleted. Launching young adults, weddings, a move, a chronically ill adult child, the removal of our foster love, the death of a family friend, the end of a friendship, financial stress, two moves in less than a year, and a physical injury had left me laid out. That tiny pill, which I prayed over before swallowing, was just enough to lend clarity and a little bit of rest I was desperately in need of.

You may never need such aid. But you are not me. What God will use to restore you is different than what He will use to restore me. And then one morning as I Weighed In, I had the gentle nudging that it was time to move on from the antidepressant. I called my doctor. She called in a lower dose, and with her instruction I was weaned off the medicine within the month. Someday I might need it again. But I trust my Creator way more than I trust my mind.

Mindful eating is a good thing. We do need to pay more attention. But the mind grows weary. It gets shut in car doors. The Holy Spirit never sleeps. Which brings me to gratitude.

Thank God, Literally

Do you have a prayer you pray before meals? We have one: "Bless us, oh Lord, and these Thy gifts, which we are about to receive from Thy bounty through Christ our Lord, amen."

If we are really hungry, we can say it in less than two seconds. Sure, we are glad we have food. Yes, we are told to give thanks. But the power of gratitude is boundless to me. In my darkest seasons, when I could not muster a prayer, I kept a gratitude journal. Every night I would list ten things I was grateful for. Some nights it was a stretch. I looked back through the journal as I prepared this section. One particularly hard day read: "(1) socks, (2) indoor plumbing, (3) Cheez-Its."

I don't remember why that day was a struggle, but apparently that was all I could muster. However, when I practice true gratitude, I can nearly feel the physical shift in my mind and body. This further supports the idea that there is power in belief. If you believe you have nothing to be thankful for, you will be sad and produce stress hormones. If you can move your mind to one of gratitude, you are focused on what you have instead of what you don't. Lacking or the worry of lack is not Beloved Living. Meghan Markle isn't worried about her lunch. Someone is bringing it. And the God who calls you His will supply every need of yours according to the riches of His glory in Christ Jesus (Philippians 4:19).

I say that calls for a "thank You!"

Bad Food?

I am guessing some of the arguments that will come up against my suggestions. "If I eat anything I want, even with a napkin in my lap, I am going to eat a metric ton of cheesecake." I would beg to differ. You might, having not really tasted and enjoyed cheesecake in years. But now that you know you will have it again, maybe even for the next four days, eventually you will want something salty or spicy. Retraining the mind might take a little while. The Weigh-In habit might be an adjustment. But how many minutes have you spent logging food, journaling, and measuring out a cup of salad? Greater, have any of the Plan Bs really set you free? You have time to make the God of your lips the God of your heart. And I know how dieting goes; it is all-consuming.

I am suggesting that you take those energies and invest them in your relationship with Jesus instead.

If you have tiny portions, perfectly measured in front of you, your mind is focused on lack and Plan B. If you have food you love, no worries it is the last time, no fear it won't be enough, and you are feasting with the Father, your heart is no longer divided. You are not lukewarm. You are just having lunch.

Shocking, I know.

And this has spilled over into every aspect of my life. And that sounds braggy because it is! I am so entirely thrilled with how much I have grown in my faith walk, I want to shout it from the rooftops. I spend less. And my decision-making is clearer. It is so fun to tap into the power of Jesus, I am undone.

Some of this was so very new, I felt so empowered, so happy. And I worried about sounding. . .um, a little like a hippie. Don't get me wrong, I have a son who is a hippie. I am a huge fan. However, in our society, especially in certain circles, there is the idea we can go too far in our "spirit-filled-ness." This is where things could turn, and all of a sudden I sound like a fruit loop or savant. It is still just me. I prayed that He would show me how to venture into this space, just as I am, and guide you to see something else He created in us.

He is so good and showed me exactly how to expound on the subject. I actually don't eat a lot of sugar. I will say that I forced myself to give up sugar. Under that law, all I thought about was sugar. I had a lot of "lasts." But under the protective cloak of Weighing In, I have gotten pretty picky. If I am going to have something sweet, say some chocolate, I don't want a Hershey bar. I want the good stuff. Without the fear of never having it again or eating fast so maybe Jesus and my body won't know I am eating outside the nature of hunger and fullness, I would rather have something I truly love. I taste my food. And satisfaction follows.

Which brings me to the visualization I worried about introducing. Our bodies hear in imagery. Now this is taught in many secular and non-Christian circles. It is the idea that by picturing what you want to happen, it happens when you imagine the outcome. There are practitioners of different teachings that achieve weight loss by merely thinking about it. And that is all well and good, but again, I have tried to save myself. It never works out.

But one of my favorite foods in the world is watermelon. Usually if I have had an intense workout, this is what I crave. And I realized while feasting with the Father that when I eat watermelon, I often have this image in my mind of my organs being drenched. I can't say it was even a deliberate image. So I sat and prayed about this. And then, I took it a step further. I take three medications in the morning, blindly. My doctor said I need this for this ailment and this one for that. But now when I Weigh In, I talk to God about my medications. As I swallow each one, I imagine the part of my body it is meant to help.

And I worried this sounded like voodoo. And then I met a woman recovering from breast cancer. She was telling me about the process of chemotherapy. She explained that her chemo nurses told her to imagine the medicine going into her body and straight to the cancer. She said they encourage patients to visualize little Pac-Men chomping away at the cancer. And then she said, "We take into our bodies these foreign substances and just assume that is all there is to it. But God created us as thinkers of images, with minds that are empowered by what we believe. Telling our bodies what to do with the medicine we are putting in our bodies guides the body to heal." And no, if we cut our hand, we don't have to visualize how to heal it. It just scabs over and gets better. But I would say, as long as we are blindly taking in whatever, we are not embracing the Helper in every aspect of our lives.

So as part of Beloved Living, I want to encourage you to do your part in investing in your wellness. Ask questions about your medications and supplements. Pray for wisdom. This is why He came to help us. He is near. . .always.

Furthermore, while I haven't talked about how many apples to eat a day or what not to eat, while in tune with your Creator, ask about the food you are eating. Are your organs being drenched in vitamins and minerals? Or do you see a lot of stagnant

Frito Pie, or dangerous chemical sweeteners, or vats of sugar? And while there is a little honeymoon phase that occurs as you transition from eating from the tree of good and evil to feasting with the Father, once you taste freedom, your body and God have suggestions that might surprise you.

I propose that you will hear Him and crave those apples and other balanced, wholesome, and delicious options He designed for you. I am experiencing this all the time now. My choices are not green juices and kale all day every day. Actually, Jesus loves me; He would never ask me to eat kale. But I do love to have green juice. Some days that is followed by a salad with real ranch dressing, because again, Jesus is a good guy. Other days it might be pizza. But what I have experienced is a balance that I don't have to record, stress, or grieve over. It is just food. I have a God. And I only need one.

Nacky

We call anything nasty in our house "nacky." Years ago one of my babies said that for nasty, and it just stuck. And before feasting with the Father, there were a lot of "nacky" things I ate because I wasn't cognizant of what I was eating. Now that I have slowed down, I am a picky eater.

I used to love Chicken McNuggets. Or at least I thought I did. I never found an eating plan that encourages the consumption of McNuggets, so in my mind they were a "bad" food. And to me, they are bad now for another reason.

I was traveling for a speaking engagement, and I pulled into a shopping center with several fast-food establishments. I prefer not to eat out of a sack, but I was in a hurry and hungry. Weighing In, I asked God what He wanted for me and was shocked and excited when I realized it was going to be McNuggets. I went inside. I ordered my food and put a napkin in my lap, prayed and gave thanks, and took a bite.

It tasted like bleach.

I tried another, same result. I ate some fries. And they were not what I remembered either. So I finished my drink, threw away the food, and got back on the road. There was an apple in my purse; that was sufficient until after the speaking engagement. The next day I was telling my friend, who was my "guinea pig" during the composition of this book. And she said, "Well, you just proved the slow down and taste part of this journey. They use bleach to make the meat of the nuggets white."

I looked into this after we hung up. I am not the boss of you, but if you like McDonald's, do not look into this. I found no evidence of bleach use, but I did find some articles about ammonia as one of the ingredients and a video of how they make McNuggets. Again I say to you, you are not going to want to watch that.

The point is simply this: what I craved was McNuggets. I had no inkling of God directing me to anything else. In the process I actually tasted what I was eating. I imagined what that looked like. There was no vitamin bath spilling over my organs. Chicken nuggets are not for me. I can have them; I don't want them. And when we are mindlessly or mindfully led, we might continue to eat things that are not the best thing for us. But when we taste what we are eating, and when we come to God asking for direction, it becomes more and more obvious what is for us and what is not.

Living Water

While I have tried my best not to be too specific about what you should and should not do, I feel it would be irresponsible for me not to talk to you about water. The first thing I want to say is this: I have no idea how much water you should drink. The second thing I am going to say is, friend, drink water.

I know. But even if you decide that this book is not for you, the very next plan you go to will tell you the same thing: drink water. Unfortunately, every single diet out there's initial success does not come from calorie restriction or ketosis or fat blocking. It comes from water loss. They all require water. That is simply because we need water to live. I can tell you how to drop ten pounds this next month, and I can promise it will work. Ready?

Drink a gallon of water a day.

You will lose weight. Granted, it is all just water, but at the same time, it is a great way to flush the body of McNuggets. I am embarrassed to tell you that at one point in my life we spent nearly two thousand dollars on medical testing on me, and my test results came back to reveal I was dehydrated.

"Mrs. Amerine, I have your lab results. I am sorry to tell you, get your things in order. You are dying. . . of thirst. That will be $1,997."

Sigh.

I am constantly on the go. I prefer iced tea. I have been known to go a whole day without food or drink because I am steeped in a creative project. But the truth is, this is part of our design. We need water. And if you need to lose weight, it will help. And if you are losing weight, fat traps toxins. Remember? I told you, fat is not a bad thing. It is protecting you from the bad stuff. When that fat depletes, those toxins are released into the body. You gotta flush them out.

When I have sought God's instruction, water is at the forefront of the direction. Sometimes when I don't want to, I say that to Him too. He knows how I am. But the conclusion is always "water."

There, I said it. If you have a problem with it, go talk to Jesus. I did not make water, and I cannot walk on water. Nor can I give you living water. But I am just going to warn you ahead of time. I don't know what or where He will take you next in this process, but seeing as how the human body, which He created, is made up of 60 percent water, I can promise He's gonna say you need some. Drink up, shoog.

A Day in the Life

I know I have bombarded you with grace, scripture,

lunacy, folly, and hopefully some wisdom. I have read enough wellness books to know, you would like to at least see what this life looks like. I will tell you what it looks like for me; but again, you have to do the "princess training" with Jesus.

I usually wake between 3:30 and 4:00. I go to bed early, but even if I don't, I am up by 4 nearly every day. I go to the bathroom, and then I get a huge container of alkaline water; we have a water cooler so the water is already cold. I think it is a 32-ounce container. I drink a lot. I'd imagine a gallon a day, but I am not legalistic about it. I pray over and take my medication. And then I get still. I may read my Bible and write in my journal. This is when I Weigh In for my exercise for the day. I suspect as I progress in my Beloved Living, this won't be important. I will just go for a walk or to yoga or dance. But now, as someone who has abused exercise, I act as if I am a recovering addict. So I seek God for this. This is also when I get inspired in my personal work as an author. I spend the next few minutes posting on my social media. Sometimes I share wisdom from my quiet time; other times I put up old or new blog posts. By the time I am finished, the morning rush will have begun. Justin packs lunches and fixes breakfast. I take Sophie to school, although she is about to get her license, so my day will have some changes. After I drop her off and say goodbye to the Vandals, and depending on where God is leading me, I either go to the gym, go for a walk, get on my exercise bike, or I don't. Either way, I will then shower and get ready.

Monday through Friday, I work upstairs in my studio or office. Except for Wednesdays. Wednesday, I work at Blakely's "art farm." My daughter Maggie and I go to the art farm and work with two or three other royalty artists. It is my favorite day of the week. Inspiration, laughter, and learning are the norm.

In the midst of all this, I drink water all day long. I Weigh In. I eat when I am hungry, and I stop when I am full. I can't tell you what that is. It varies. If there is a birthday, I might have cake. If Justin got a run on napa cabbage, praise the Lord! We have Chinese chicken salad. Sometimes I skip a meal or fast. But I am not doing this to "make" God do something. I do it for clarity. Sometimes I do it as worship. Other times I feel the nudging I should, so I Weigh In. I talk to God about my motives, and the Holy Spirit is my nourishment.

After a full day, kids wander in. We do homework and eat dinner as a family. I like to take a bath before bed. I am usually in bed by 8 or 8:30. There I write in my journal again. I list my Gains for the day and things I am grateful for. Weekends are laxer, but I do not neglect this Sacred Standard, the Weigh In: I Want to Experience God and Holy Instruction. Always. In everything. Which brings me to this place.

This is my life. I am not built like you. We don't have the same careers, demands, or tastes. My life's calling is not the same as yours. Really the greatest thing we have in common is a God who loved us unto

His death so we might live. This is the Good News. This is the plan that won't fail you. I can only tell you for certain, there is only room in your heart for one God, no matter what size your pants are.

Well, Girl Wisdom

I can't tell you what to eat or when to eat it. I can't tell you how to move. And I cannot make you believe. You will have to experience it for yourself. Take a moment and imagine what this would look like for you, His princess. Write out what you want. Ask Him how to get there. And then, wait for His answer. I am not afraid to promise you, He will.

Freedom Gain

No other God. No more wasted time or money. Plan A, Weighing In, Gains instead of losses, and Beloved Living is yours. Congratulations, Beloved.

Conclusion

*A*nd here we are. I can't say that I am out of all the things there are to say about this. Too much has happened. I have so much freedom and peace, I could go on for another four chapters.

I pray you are not afraid to let Him be your only answer, but I get it. I know it is scary to stop thinking "diet" and start eating real food just because you are hungry and it sounds good. If you feel like you need more science, I would recommend the book *Intuitive Eating* by Elyse Resch and Evelyn Tribole and the book *You're Not Sick, You're Thirsty* by F. Batmanghelidj. But I would follow those recommendations with this prompting: this won't be the last book you read. But while we are never separated from the love of God, if you add even a touch of the law, you are no longer experiencing grace.

Grace is everything.

Our marine son, John, was deployed for nine months. When he returned home, he had wonderful stories about all the things he saw all around the world. But he also had some very hard things to report. One of which was a village in Africa where young girls were standing beneath walls with a price spray-painted over their heads. This is a horrific image. It breaks my heart; it broke John's. And there are organizations out there doing amazing work in the world of sex trafficking and sex slavery. I pray that influence grows.

But as I wrote this, that image continued to flash in my mind. The battle cry is "Break them out! Save them from that horrible existence!" But when the organizations do break these women and children out, they also train them to do something else to provide for themselves. All they have ever known is slavery.

So if you snuck out in the middle of the night and set them free, without direction or a vocation, they would probably have no choice but to continue to sell themselves on the streets. Now imagine, someone came along and saved them from that life and took them to a safe house, provided them with an education, clothes, fine food, and everything they needed for a life of peace and happiness.

Sounds good. I would do it if I could. But now, imagine that one of the girls, who had everything she needed, would climb out the window of her safe room every night and go back to that dirty wall, that crude price spray-painted above her head. One would have to ask why anyone would do that. It makes no sense.

But I did it for years. When I said yes to Jesus, He set me free from the slavery of the law. The veil was torn, He calls me friend, and although He offered me everything, I kept looking for another master. Someone to keep me in line, to control me, and step into my life and onto His throne. Back in the garden, the sneaky snake whispers, "But if you just were better, here try this." I grappled with this conclusion. I know the back copy of this book says it is funny. I hope some of it was. But more, I hope that you are free and you will never go back to that wall of slavery.

Once you are set free, you are free indeed. And once that happens, we are no longer burdened with self. We have only one God and that God, who has plans and a future for us, can direct us vividly in ways to glorify His kingdom, spread the Good News, and set captives free. As hard as it was to admit so much of my folly, I can boldly say, I wanted nothing more than to tell of His goodness. And although there are physical benefits and tangible gains to this way of living and eating, even if there had not been, His grace is always sufficient.

Your life's work, the reason you were created, was not to conquer weight loss or fitness. You are more than a number on the scale or pants size. Do not let the enemy rob you of the intimacy that comes when you love God with all that you are.

And so I close with this. Where will He take you? Who might He lead you to set free in His name? What impact will you have as His hands and feet when you are no longer shackled and the only god you worship is the God with no beginning and no end?

Stay in the palace, dear one. Don't sneak out. Do not look for any Savior other than the One who died for you. He is all-consuming. He is more than enough. He is everything.

Enjoy the feast before you, my friend. It will be

like nothing you have ever tasted before. Welcome to the banquet hall, taste and see, princess. . . .

Jesus be all over you.

Love,
Jami

Acknowledgments

To You, my Lord Jesus—friend, healer, redeemer. I like You.

Special thanks to my family.

Justin, you are simply the best. Thank you for loving us all so well. Thank you for all that you do. It is amazing. You are my very best friend. . .and you aren't hard to look at either.

Maggie, Christian, John, Anne, Luke, Sophie, Sam, and Charlie, you are all my favorite.

Mom and Dad, thank you for liking me so much.

Stacey and Dean, Michael and Kelly, and the pixies and Vandals, thank you for your prayers and support. You are most dear to me.

To my friends and sisters Kim Phelan, Marcy Toppert, Lorraine Reep, Tracy Steel, Jeane Wynn, Shelby Spear, Crystal Paine, Christy Mobley, Emily Potter, and Christine Carter—your prayers, friendship, and wisdom have made me better. Thank you.

To Katie and Adam Reid, thank you for your continued support and love. Katie, thank you for making me "well-er-est."

To Carey Scott. . .where were you the first 44 years of my life? I like you, friend.

Lorraine Reep my first "fan". . .I love you.

To Blakely Bering, I sure do like you. I have been

richly blessed by your vision. I have been forever changed by your friendship.

To my friends at the Art Farm—Wednesdays are my favorite.

To my Facebook tribe, I would be nowhere without you. Thank you for reading my words and caring about my life. I see you too. Jesus be all over you.

For Jessica Kirkland, my friend and agent, thank you for your friendship and determination. You are my busiest friend.

Kelly McIntosh, Shalyn Sattler, and everyone at Barbour Publishing, this was the most fun. It was an honor to write this with you. You guys are pretty cool.